THE ART OF GROWING

THE
ART
OF
GROWING

*A Guide to
Psychological Maturity*

ROBERT E. NIXON, M.D.
VASSAR COLLEGE

RANDOM HOUSE
NEW YORK

155.5
NIXO

To Helen and Abby

PREFACE

Some people seem to believe that the best way to bring a rose to maturity is to pluck it, while still a bud, and then to press it in the family Bible. In disagreeing with this view I cannot be tolerant enough to say that it is simply an honest difference of opinion. So far as I am concerned, these people are dead wrong, and I am dedicated to rescuing as many buds as possible from the press before it is too late; to replacing them on nutritive stems; and then to giving them the opportunity to bring themselves to maturity. Of course, one's efforts are not always timely, and not all buds want to be rescued, but the effort must be made, regardless, if one's convictions are strong.

This book is a primitive effort, it is doubtless a crude effort, and it certainly will fail to reach as many young people as I should like it to reach. But at this particular moment it is the best effort of which I am capable. And anyway, any effort is better than empty complaining. With this book I am reaching toward the potential for growth that exists in all youth. How many will be disposed to respond I have no real idea. In so reaching it is inevitable that I shall tread on unsuspecting and more-or-less innocent toes; and again, how many of their possessors will be disposed to respond I have no real idea. The responsibility, however, in both instances, is mine and mine alone, despite a list of acknowledgments that is long indeed for such a thin book.

First of all, I am indebted to my wife. She not only exhibited her usual most generous wealth of wifely virtues during the months when the book was the principal occupant of my head, but in addition provided encouragement, untold hours of conversation without which the book could never have been realized, and constructive criticism very much beyond the call of duty. And further, during revisions of the manuscript, she supplied suggestions, turns of phrase, and even paragraphs without which the book would have been a weak vessel indeed.

Second, I am indebted to Vassar College for providing me, during the last ten years, with a setting of academic freedom that could not have been bettered. The administration left me to my own devices, to see what I could see, to interpret it as I would, to do with it what I could, with no strings attached, no pressures applied, no preconceptions, no institutional demands. Without such a setting of freedom the book could not have been conceived.

Third, I am indebted to the students of Vassar College who have seen fit to consult me, to let me listen to them and learn from them, during these ten years. More than they know, they have been my teachers. And without them and their generous trust the book could not have been.

Fourth, I am indebted to my friends and colleagues of the Vassar faculty, both for an informal liberal arts education acquired for the most part over innumerable lunch tables, and for specific critical assistance with the thinking that preceded, and the writing that resulted in, the book. Most particularly I wish to acknowledge the help and encouragement provided me by Professors Dwight Chapman and L. Joseph Stone.

Fifth, I am indebted to many young people of my acquaintance, both Vassar students and others, who read early versions of the manuscript. Their comments, criticisms, and suggestions have been most helpful and constructive during the arduous business of revision and finishing.

And finally I am deeply indebted to a paragon among secretaries, Edna Durbeck, who has not only managed my office affairs most capably during these years and done all the typing necessary for several versions of the manuscript, but who has managed as well to learn to read my writing.

CONTENTS

Introduction

Someone has said, "You're only young once, but once is enough if you work it right." Beneath the humor of the comment is a kernel of truth—there *is* work to be done while one is young, and it needs to be done right. It is my intention with this book to provide youth with a guide that may facilitate "working it right" so that once will, in fact, be enough. The work to which I refer is the process of psychological growth, and its aim is the achievement of *true* or *psychologically mature* adulthood. By youth I mean specifically the years from about seventeen to twenty-two. My basic premise is that young people who undertake the psychological work characteristic of the years of youth can achieve a state of psychological maturity by their middle twenties.

This premise requires defense, and its terms call for definition. In the popular view the years of youth are "the best years of your life." They are considered years of happiness, of light-heartedness, of gaiety and fun, of a relative absence of responsibility; they commonly appear to constitute the last fling before the onset of adulthood with its work, its routine, its drab, responsibility-laden succession of days and weeks and months and years, each like all the others. This view owes its popularity to the large number of adults who have forgotten the facts of their own youth and for whom the years of adulthood are less than fulfilling, less than xiv / THE ART OF GROWING

satisfying. I have no doubt that a close relationship exists between their forgetfulness and their lack of fulfillment; not having done what I call the *work* of youth, they cannot fully enjoy the possibilities of adulthood; not having *used* youth, they remember it inaccurately and nostalgically as a time of unmitigated pleasure, a pleasant, irresponsible time to which they would like to return. For them, once has not been enough.

My view of youth, in contrast, is that it comprises possibly the most difficult period in the entire cycle of human life. It is the time during which one needs to leave childhood behind and enter adulthood; it is a time, at best, of arduous transition from a comfortable but temporary state of dependent existence to one that is independent and permanent—until it is ended by death. And it is a transition for which most young people are not prepared, a transition for which there seem to exist no guidelines.

I hasten to add that this unconventional view of the nature of youth is not mine alone. All good teachers share it, in fact all mature adults share it. And what is more important, the majority of young people with whom I have worked as a college psychiatrist share it. In short, it is a rather widely recognized view, and if it is outweighed by the ubiquity of the popular view it is nevertheless deserving of examination. But before subjecting it to closer scrutiny, I should like to say a few words concerning the young people I have known who espouse it. At the outset, I must say that they are people who are at once admirable and difficult to live with. They are admirable because of their courage, their tenacity, their boundless curiosity concerning both themselves and their world, their unremitting use of the critical faculty, their insistence upon using their minds to correlate what they feel with what they know with what they do. They are difficult to live with because of their relentless questioning of almost everything that enters their ken, and because of their equally relentless demand that their questions be answered. They do not rest much, and they do not make it possible for the adults who deal with them—their teachers and parents, for example—to rest much either. They are impatient, they are in a great hurry, they are blind to every issue but *the* issue of the moment, they quibble and argue and debate and object. They reduce their adult friends to weariness, and at the same time, paradoxically, they make them feel young. These young people, in short, are *working* their way through the years of youth, and if their demands on the adults in their world are great, their demands on themselves are vastly greater. From the adults they demand answers; from themselves they demand growth. They expect the adults to *show* them the way, but they expect themselves to get there. Speaking as an adult who has spent much time with such young people, I can attest that they are more than merely stimulating—they are downright invigorating. Where they are, there is Life. I shall refer to these young people as "growers."

Unfortunately, such people as these do not make up the whole of youth. Two other groups are readily discernible, and while they may be less trying to adults they are also less stimulating. In fact, sooner or later they become only boring. The larger of these groups is made up of *conformers*. These are the young people who agree with the popular view of youth. What their elders say, they accept. If youth is supposed to be "the best years of your life," then it *is*. If they are told to behave themselves, or to think of others, or to study, or to work hard, they simply do as they are told. If they are told that all Negroes are lazy, then all Negroes *are* lazy. If, in contrast, they are told that all whites are domineering, then all whites *are* domineering. They never ask "Why?" or "How?" or "What's your proof?" —they only say "Yes" to everything. They make no demands, they are usually popular, they are more often than not "successful," but they are dull. They do not seem to *work* their way through the years of youth, but rather to *agree* their way through.

The other nonworking group is made up of the *rebels*. These are young people who are so diametrically opposed to the conformers that the more closely they are examined, the less apparent their differences. The one group says "Yes" to everything, the other says "No." The conformer says, "The world I have inherited is all right, and I will go along with it." The rebel says, "The world I have inherited is all wrong, and I will go along with none of it." They seem worlds apart, and yet they are in one sense identical: neither expects anything of himself, at least not anything resembling responsibility. For the one the attitude is "The world is good, so I will accept it"; and for the other, "The world is bad, so I will reject it." Both these views stand in marked contrast to that of the growers: for them, a question takes the place of a statement. Their question is "What is the world, who am I, and what can *I* do about both?"

Obviously, I am oversimplifying when I use such terms as "grower," "rebel," and "conformer." In everyone some psychological growth occurs, even without his own personal cooperation, and for each of us there is more than enough to rebel against, and quite a good deal worth conforming to. But it is necessary to stress some differences: the grower is interested in his own growth; he knows—or is learning—how and when and why to rebel, how and when and why to conform. The rebel does not concern himself with his own growth, but with his objections to the world. In his own social circle of fellow-rebels he is a remarkable conformer. And the conformer, too, pays little or no attention to his own growth: he is comfortable in the passive acceptance of whatever he has been given. This is oversimplification, and typing of human beings is at best a risky business. It tends to assign people to arbitrary niches from which they feel they cannot escape, and although it may provide a rough frame of reference, a way of classifying things that are generally true, it is rarely specifically applicable. My reason for resorting to it is that it does clarify discussion, but only if it is carefully qualified.

Until fairly recently we believed that virtually all young people were either rebels or conformers. The few who apparently fitted neither of these common patterns were viewed as odd, or especially gifted, or artistic, or highly talented, or even as geniuses; but whatever their distinguishing characteristics, they seemed to be so very few as to be without statistical significance. The "average" youth appeared to be either a rebel or a conformer, and "average" was synonymous with "normal." "Abnormals," under the terms of that scheme, included those young people who were not "adjusted" to the social setting of the others—the extremely rebellious, the extremely conforming, and of course the small group that belonged to neither camp.

But during the last twenty-five years we have gradually come to realize that the earlier notion about the normality of youth was not merely misleading; it was inaccurate. We know now that the apparently specially gifted young people, those neither rebellious nor conforming, whose number seemed to be so small that they could be conveniently overlooked, are the psychologically normal among youth, and that the larger groups, the rebels and conformers, are less than normal. For a people with so firm a reliance upon, and belief in, the will of the majority, it is difficult to imagine or to accept a distinction between "average" and "normal," but the distinction nevertheless must be made. In ten years as a college psychiatrist I have listened to, and talked with, more than 10 per cent of a student population the cumulative total of which is by now nearly 15,000. Of the 1500 I have known, at least 60 per cent, or 900, have been growers—that is, normal, neither rebels nor conformers. I should guess that an equal number of growers in that student population did not cross my path, and if my guess is an approximation of reality the total number of *normal* young people in the college, over the past ten years, would come to 1800, more or less, or about 12 per cent. This is a good-sized minority that certainly cannot be overlooked, and from it I have learned to make the distinction between the normal and the less-than-normal.[1]

A. H. Maslow, a psychologist, after a rather detailed discussion of common misuses of the concept of psychological normality, says " . . . We have come closer to identifying it (the normal) with the highest excellence of which we are capable . . . This ideal is not an unattainable goal set out far ahead of us; rather it is actually within us, existent but hidden, as potentiality rather than as actuality." [2] And James Thurber, in his last published piece, wrote, "We are assured, by some authorities, that the normal is a matter of mass behavior, but the normal can never be synonymous with the average, the majority, the customary, or the habitual. *The normal is that which functions in accordance with its design.* . . ." (italics mine)[3] The youth who is psychologically normal, then, is the one who realizes his potentiality for excellence, who functions in accordance with his psychological design, and the youth who is less than normal does not so function.

But just what constitutes the psychological design of youth? Thanks again to the college students I have worked with during these years, I have come to believe that the psychological capability characteristic of the years of youth is the *cognitive* capacity[1]—the capacity for knowing oneself and one's setting in an objective and detached fashion. This capacity appears to reach its maturity two or three years after puberty—at, say, fourteen to sixteen. Once it has developed, the young person is able to "see" or know himself and his world. The youth who attempts to utilize this new capacity, who functions in accordance with his design, is a grower, whereas the one who does not choose to utilize it, or who utilizes only that aspect of it which has to do with knowing his setting, is either a conformer or a rebel. The first is normal, even though he belongs to a minority, and the others are less-than-normal, despite their inclusion in the majority.

Some confusion may attend my use of two inter-locking classifications: normal versus less-than-normal, growers versus rebels and conformers. I feel bound to introduce both classifications, since each plays its own specific and important part in my thesis. The first tells us where we stand in theoretical terms, and allows for optimism concerning the progress of young people toward the normal; and the second suggests the nature of the main identifying characteristics that occur in "real" life. In using the second classification I do not mean to imply that if the label fits, its possessor is stuck with it. Quite the contrary: I am discussing the achievement of psychological normality, a goal I hold to be attainable, and any starting place is a good one. Rebels and conformers can become growers. Neither need remain static.

In my basic premise I referred to the psychological work characteristic of the years of youth, and now it should be clear that I am speaking of the work asso-ciated with the utilization of the cognitive capacity. It is not particularly easy to be cognitive, to strive for an objective and reasonably detached view of oneself and one's setting. The growers see the years of youth as a time of work, of struggle, of study, of questioning. I do not wish to give the impression that they are always grim, sweating, and mirthless—certainly they have at least as much fun as the others, and they know what it means to be adventurous[4]—but the achievement of *growth* is their primary motive and they work at it assiduously much of the time. This growth—or any other growth, for that matter—involves the building of something new upon that which has been earlier established; and when I refer to it as *psychological work* I mean to imply that it is growth in the psychological sphere, that it consists of *thinking* about one's self and the world in which one lives, and that it can be pursued deliberately and willingly—it can be worked at—by the person involved. In other words, it is not something that must be left to chance or to accident or the passage of time: it is a matter that can be approached and tackled knowingly and purposefully.

This is work that is familiar to the grower, and it is because work is an inherent part of psychological growth that I have entitled this book *The Art of Growing*. Erich Fromm, in his excellent book *The Art of Loving* (the similarity of titles attests to my debt to Fromm) makes the point that "love is an art, just as living is an art; if we want to learn how to love we must proceed in the same way we have to proceed if we want to learn any other art, say music, painting, carpentry, or the art of medicine or engineering." He goes on to say that learning an art involves mastery of its theory and practice, and the conviction that ". . . there must be nothing else in the world more important than the art." [5] These remarks are as true of growth as they are of love, and they show clearly the relationship between work and growing.

But if growing is an art, does this not introduce the question of *talent*? As with painting or music or writing, are not some people more talented for growing than others? At first glance it would seem so—I have already described growers and non-growers—but on closer examination it becomes clear that success or failure in psychological growth is not truly a matter of talent. After all, anyone can *think* if he only will, but not everyone can draw or sing. More precisely, it is a function of *freedom*. The individual who is free to grow grows, and works while doing it, whereas the one who is not free fails to grow, or at least grows less. The forces limiting that freedom may be internal or external: the young person who does not know that growth is possible is internally limited, the one who must bend every effort merely to survive in the physical sense is externally limited. But in either case limitations can be lifted, freedom can supervene—and then growth will occur.

In other words, in all living matter there exists a powerful inherent potentiality for self-correction, for normalization, for movement from the less-than-normal toward the normal. In the human animal this potentiality can be worked at and utilized, utilized and enjoyed. For example, a farmer of my acquaintance, well into his eighties, was finally forced by his aging heart to give up the dawn-to-dusk routine of heavy work he had always known. Consigned to his ancient Morris chair, he could do nothing but look out the window at his farmyard. One morning, after two or three weeks of chair-sitting, he greeted me, his eyes bright with discovery, with "Hey, young feller, I had a dream last night, and I been a-thinkin' about it this mornin'. Seems like I'm a *thinkin'* feller!" Freed finally from the limitations imposed by a lifetime of physical work, he was able to recognize his ability to do mental work, and he was delighted with his discovery. Talent is not an issue when we concern ourselves with the art of growing, or the art of loving, or the art of living. These are all examples of art with a small *a*, and in this sense art means work, together with a consuming interest. Formal Art, with a capital A, means work, a consuming interest, and talent in large quantities; but this is not the sense in which I am using the word here.

Interestingly, the idea of youth as a time for work is implicit in the behavior and words of the conformers and rebels, too. Both groups *deny* specifically the issues the growers are concerned with. Conformers tend to reinforce the denial by working very hard to be "good" young people, according to the tenets and beliefs of their elders, and rebels reinforce the denial by working very hard to be "bad." Both groups, however unknowingly, actually do *work* their way through youth, usually with substantially more expenditure of energy than the growers; and if their work is subverted or perverted, or fruitless, it is still work. Fortunately, it can be transformed into the work of growth.

In my basic premise I said that the grower can achieve a state of psychological maturity in his middle twenties. If he does the psychological work of youth, if he takes advantage of his new ability to examine himself and his world, he will have achieved a sense of independent, individual, and unique personal identity. This is more than the common notion of identity that is based only upon role, position, and place of residence, and that gives rise to such shallow self-identification as "I am John Jones. I am an engineer. I live in Chicago and I have two children." Rather, this is a sense of identity that makes it possible for the grower to say, without braggadocio, "I am fairly sure I know who I am and what I am. I know what I like and dislike, I know what I can do, I know what I cannot do." He will also have achieved a view of the world that makes it possible for him to say, and without cynicism, "I am beginning to know what kind of a place the world is. I think I know what's good about it, I think I know what's bad about it." Putting the two together, he then lives his life in such a fashion that he enjoys and utilizes the good aspects of his world and does what he can to rectify the bad. This way of life, in my view, constitutes psychological maturity, and I hold it to be achievable by anyone who will accept the challenge and the opportunity of youth.

There are those who will object that no one can truly "know" himself, that at best we can only approach the goal of self-knowledge but never actually reach it. In their way they are of course right: but just as a person can get to know a great city, such as New York, well enough to avoid getting lost, and then devote his adult life to the discovery and exploration of its ever-changing details, so he can come to know himself well enough to avoid getting lost, by his mid-twenties if he works at it, and then during the rest of his life discover and explore the ever-changing details of his own identity. Others will object that this thesis makes no allowance for the unusually early maturer—the prodigy, for example, who appears to have "grown up" by, say, seventeen or eighteen. Certainly there are exceptionally gifted young people whose mastery of a talent is essentially mature at that age, and without question there are many young people whose mastery of social roles is virtually complete that early, too. But in neither case are we discussing *psychological* maturity, a goal that can be achieved only through a specific kind of work that takes time. And finally there are some who will object that I am consigning youth to a lengthy transition, to a "phase" in which everything feels tentative and nothing seems permanent or durable. This is almost precisely my view of youth, so this book itself will have to be my defense. Of course permanent and enduring principles are forged, and binding decisions are made, in the course of youth; but the grower does not commit himself irretrievably until he has questioned, examined, and tested, as fully as he can, every available alternative.

Psychological maturity, in other words, is a way of living one's life. Possession of a clear, objective, and undistorted view of oneself is necessary to psychological maturity, but by itself it is not enough. Possession of an equally clear, objective, and undistorted view of the world one lives in is also necessary, but by itself it is not enough, either; and the two together, moreover, are still not sufficient to constitute psychological maturity. A life lived meaningfully in the presence of, and with reference to, these two views is what constitutes psychological maturity. More words have been written in description of what psychological maturity is *not* than in definition of what it *is*. All authorities agree, however, at least by implication, on these three elements: knowledge of self, knowledge of one's setting, and some sort of active living that makes sense in the framework provided by that knowledge.[6] I wish to add only one more suggestion: if psychological maturity is to be purposeful, deliberate, controlled, and rational, rather than accidental, then the knowledge of self and of setting needs to be conscious and explicit. And it is precisely here that we encounter the psychological work of youth. As I have already said, it is work—sometimes devilishly hard work, but much of the time also exhilarating and exciting work—to discover what one really is, as opposed to what one is allegedly supposed to be; and it is work, too, to discover what the world actually is. Psychological growth, during the years of youth, consists in making and following up these discoveries. Psychological *maturity* occurs as the grower begins to *live* with these discoveries. Since each "self" is made up of a unique collection of capacities and limitations, interests and lacks of interest, appetites and aversions, it follows that no two examples of psychological maturity are identical, that no two growers will achieve precisely the same end, that no one can dictate to anyone else the shape of his or her way of life. Each grower, in short, must do his own work of definition and discovery, each will reach his own particular goal, his own special way of life, his own variety of maturity.

No one knows, with any precision, how many young

people actually do undertake the work of growth, but my own guess is that the average would fall somewhere between 10 and 15 per cent of contemporary American youth. Further, I believe the percentage is increasing, and that it is higher than it has ever been before. As a group, these young people evade notice because they do not flock together like the conformers and the rebels. They have more tolerance for loneliness, for isolation; they are less dependent upon the tranquilizing effect of herd membership; and since they belong to a group that is not commonly recognized, each of them suspects that he is not only unique, but also something of an outsider. Consequently they generally do not expect to be identified as members of a group.

But a group they are, and a group whose importance is greater than its numbers would suggest. So far as I can determine, the world has never before undergone such rapid and sweeping change as it has in the past forty or fifty years; and if humanity is to survive its own capacity for wreaking change, it must develop some considerable ability for living with it. I contend it is precisely this ability that the growers are striving to master. Conformers learn to accept change, simply because it exists, and to adjust to it uncritically. Rebels learn to encourage still more change, simply because it is different from what preceded it, and their encouragement of change is uncritical. It is only the growers who learn to be critical, who learn that change is not necessarily progress, that though it is inevitable it comes in two flavors, good and bad. I suspect that they hold the fate and the future of humanity in their hands. Their responsibility is awful, their opportunity boundless.

Obviously, being a grower seems to be a pretty rigorous career. Many will ask, "Why go to the trouble? Why not enjoy the last fling of freedom from responsibility and play my way through these years?" Others will ask, "Why make such an issue of it? Why not just muddle through and hope for the best?" And indeed these choices exist. But if the sense of identity is not earned, then neither is the objective view of the world earned, nor can a way to live meaningfully in that world be learned. The world already has so many bad features, ranging from war, pestilence, and famine to billboards and tailfins, that in occasional moments of discouragement one fails to see how it could have more. But then another school is closed to prevent integration, or another bomb is tested, or another river overflows its banks in China. If enough people persist in enjoying freedom without responsibility long enough, there will be, too soon, no freedom left to enjoy, and perhaps not even people to regret its passing. The wrong choice is there for the taking, and many will take it. They will avoid the rigors of growth, and the pains that go with it, but they will not grow. They will become adult in name only, more or less practiced and fluent in adult roles, but emotionally still children, still dependent, still helpless. They will accept the status quo unthinkingly, or they will go through the empty motions of fighting it, only to replace it with another that is no better. One way or the other, they will "adjust" themselves, as painlessly and uncritically as possible, to a world sorely in need of constructive criticism and improvement, in a country that is at once the world's richest and in many respects the world's sickest. They will look back at youth as the best years of their lives and regret its passing, they will be bored and dissatisfied with adulthood. We can only hope they will not be too many, that we and our children will not be among the last examples of a short-lived, big-brained, self-destructive species of primate.

Some, however, will take the right choice. Some will decide to go to the trouble of growing. They will find no dearth of trouble: on occasion they will wish they hadn't started, they will sometimes feel in the depth of despair, they may be ridiculed by the cool and the clever, they will often be alone and lonely. But sometimes they will feel an exhilaration, a joy, unknowable and unimaginable to the cool; they will discover the pleasure of discovery, the strength of independence, the privacy and richness of thought, the satisfaction of accomplishment. And they will know the incomparable warmth and meaningfulness of sharing the search with a few kindred spirits. They will learn the importance of tears and laughter and sweat and possibly of blood, they will become intimately familiar with their own mistakes, triumphs, convictions, and feelings, with their own capacities and limitations. They will be capable of intimate familiarity with someone else, they will be able to love the world where it deserves love and to fight it effectively where it is hateful. In short, eventually they will earn, by their own efforts, their human birthright— no one can give it to them.

This book is for anyone who wishes to make the right choice, the hard choice. It cannot materially shorten or lighten the transition from childhood to adulthood, it makes no effort to teach the techniques or roles of adulthood, it cannot give anyone his—or her— sense of identity, and it most certainly cannot tell anyone how to live his own life. At best it can only provide some pointers, clues, and hints; it can discuss and illustrate and perhaps clarify some of the ways in which one may endeavor to seek his own identity, and it can indicate some of the sore points of this world we all share. And identification of the sore points is a process to which we adults have devoted neither time enough, dedication enough, nor honesty enough. This is understandable since the world as it presently exists is of our making; but it is also inexcusable, since we brought our youth into it without asking their permission. In this area I shall be speaking for myself, inevitably, and my view of the world may not be agreeable to everyone of my own generation. I can only say that I shall endeavor to be as courageous and honest in my criticism of our world as I should like youth to be in its appraisal of itself, and of us.

Erik Erikson has written, "If we will only learn to let live, the plan for growth is all there." [7] Growing is an art, an art that depends upon work in a setting of freedom. I hope this book will contribute to an increase in freedom from misconceptions, misinformation, and insupportable myth concerning the nature of man and his growth, and the world he lives in; for the more freedom of this sort we possess, the more we "let live," and the more we let live the more we grow. Here, then, is a rough guide to psychological maturity drawn by a member of a left-over generation. The youthful generation, with the vigor of its years, will have to do its own growing. To its members I bid Godspeed, and best wishes.[8]

REFERENCES

1. R. E. Nixon, "An Approach to the Dynamics of Growth in Adolescence." *Psychiatry*, 24:1 (Feb., 1961).
2. A. H. Maslow, *Motivation and Personality*. New York, Harper and Brothers, 1954, p. 352.
3. James Thurber, "The Future, if Any, of Comedy." *Harper's Magazine*, 223:1339 (Dec., 1961), p. 44.

4. The young person I call a grower has been called by
Heath *The Reasonable Adventurer* (S. Roy Heath,
"The Reasonable Adventurer and Others—A Two Factor Model of Ego Functioning," *Journal of Counselling
Psychology*, 6:1, 3-14, 1959). In my paper cited in
Reference no. 1, above, I referred to this sort of youth
as the "Acceptor," meaning that he accepted the capacity for self-cognition. I have since rejected that term
because of its obvious connotative similarity to the term
"Complier." Anna Freud describes late adolescence as
a time of struggle (Anna Freud, "Adolescence," *The
Psychoanalytic Study of the Child*, International Univer-
sities Press, Vol. XIII, 1958, p. 255), and the concept
of the grower is familiar and even well known to many
college psychiatrists and psychologists. Unfortunately,
however, this is a matter of common knowledge *within*
the field, rather than one that has enjoyed publication.
Among those who have described and/or discussed the
adult form of the grower are Riesman, with his Au-
tonomous Man (D. Riesman, *The Lonely Crowd*, New
Haven, The Yale University Press, 1950); Fromm, with
his Productive Orientation (Erich Fromm, *Man for
Himself*, New York, Rinehart and Co., 1947); Maslow,
with his Self-actualizer (A. H. Maslow, *Motivation and
Personality*, New York, Harper and Brothers, 1954);
Murphy, with his fusion of the "three natures of man"
(G. Murphy, *Human Potentialities*, New York, Basic
Books, 1958); May, with his conscious self (Rollo May,
Man's Search for Himself, New York, W. W. Norton
and Co., 1950); Allport's Proprium (Gordon Allport,
Becoming, New Haven, Yale University Press, 1955);
Horney's Actual Self (J. L. Rubins, "Notes on the
Organization of the Self," *American Journal of Psycho-
analysis*, 18:171, 1958) and Rado's Biocultural Acting
Self (S. Rado, "From the Metapsychological Ego to the
Biocultural Acting Self," *Journal of Psychology*, 46;277-
285, 1958). Perhaps the most important theoretical
basis for contemporary study of psychological develop-
ment during adolescence is that contributed by Erik
Erikson. One of the best statements of his develop-

mental position occurs in his *Childhood and Society*, New York, W. W. Norton and Co., 1950.

5. Erich Fromm, *The Art of Loving*. New York, Harper and Brothers, 1956, p. 5.

6. Most discussions of what I refer to as psychological maturity appear under the heading of Mental Health. For a definitive exposition of present-day thought concerning the concept of mental health see M. Jahoda, *Current Concepts of Positive Mental Health*, New York, Basic Books, 1958. For an excellent extended essay on the subject, one which is nonscientific but humanistic, knowing, and literate, see Joseph Wood Krutch, *Human Nature and the Human Condition*, New York, Random House, 1959.

7. Erik Erikson, Growth and Crises of the "Healthy Personality," in C. Kluckhohn, H. A. Murray, and D. M. Schneider, eds., *Personality in Nature, Society, and Culture*. New York, Alfred A. Knopf, 1953, p. 225.

8. It is quite possible that this book will be greeted with objections by colleagues on the grounds that it constitutes a premature effort to disseminate specialized knowledge. Such objections are readily justifiable—the study of psychological growth and development in middle and late adolescence is a very young field. Certainly no one can speak yet with unquestioned authority in this area, and we are still far from sharing even a common vocabulary and from agreeing on terms and definitions. There is no question but that this field of inquiry is undergoing extremely rapid development at the moment; new ground is hardly broken before another plow penetrates on the other side of the next fence. It would be professionally more graceful, and unquestionably technically easier, to postpone the writing of a book like this until the field is more stable; but it is my impression that neither time nor youth is willing to wait. Consequently I am knowingly sacrificing finesse in the interests of matching supply with demand. Obviously such a choice means that this book will be crude, primitive, and destined for early obsolescence; but despite these difficulties I remain convinced that we are at a point

in history where a less than ideal book for youth is better than no book at all. In any event, I am confident that whatever misinformation resides herein will prove to be relatively harmless and, indeed, ignored by young people who are trying to grow. They are not characterized by gullibility.

THE ART OF GROWING

1

Out of the Family, Into the World

In an earlier day, books written for youth frequently referred to birds and bees, but the parallels drawn between these creatures and the human adolescent served
the Victorian tastes of society better than they served
the curiosity of the young. However, one hesitates to
break a grand tradition, so in spite of the questionable
usefulness of the birds-and-bees analogy I shall begin
this book with one featuring the butterfly. A new
butterfly, fresh out of the cocoon, is a pathetic creature
whose first attempts at life seem to show little promise.
He—or she—stands unsteadily on shaky legs, moving
his wings, still damp and not yet entirely unfurled, in
a slow up-and-down motion. To the human observer of
this uncertain start in life the butterfly's feeble efforts
may convey no hint of the beautiful free flight soon to
come. Indeed, the observer may consider the butterfly a
mildly repulsive and thoroughly inadequate bug, lose
interest in the scene, and miss the magic of the first
floating flight, minutes later, of the adult butterfly.

Unavoidably, the young human being is in the same vulnerable state at the beginning of youth. He has emerged from a social incubator, rather than from a cocoon; it is the area behind his ears, rather than his wings, that seems damp; and the time sequence of his transition is measured in years, rather than minutes. But, like the new butterfly, his legs are shaky, he lacks experience, he does not yet know how to "fly." And undoubtedly he is seen by some older human observers as mildly repulsive and inadequate. Not all of them have the patience to wait for him to take off.

Having paid my respects to tradition I shall now leave the butterfly to his summer and move on to mention an aspect of human life that is specifically human, an aspect that gives rise, directly or indirectly, to all the growing pains the human animal experiences between the beginning of youth and the achievement of adulthood. This specifically human capacity distinguishes us sharply from the rest of the animal kingdom, and it can perhaps best be identified by calling it *awareness*.[1] Because of his capacity for awareness the human being cannot simply emerge from the incubator and let it go at that. Rather, having emerged, he will find himself both looking back at the incubator in an effort to discover in what sort of place he spent all that time, and looking at *himself* in an effort to discover what sort of creature he is. This momentous emergence seems to occur most commonly at around fifteen or sixteen. It can occur a little earlier or a little later, but whenever it occurs it seldom becomes visible and conscious to the young person involved, at least in our culture, until eighteen or nineteen or later. Many eighteen-year-olds refer back to the time of emergence with such statements as "That was when I first began to think," or "I don't think I really *knew* anything until I was fifteen," or "I didn't realize my parents were *people* until I was about sixteen."

Emergence from the incubator is characterized by a bit of growing pain, by some manifestation of emotional discomfort. It may take the form of moodiness, increased shyness, quick embarrassment, depression, rebelliousness, a feeling of tension. Not infrequently it takes physical form with headaches, stomach-aches, loss of appetite or increased appetite, certain types of skin disorder, menstrual irregularities, changes in sleep patterns. But whatever its form, the discomfort is the result of the emotional state known as *anxiety*. Anxiety is the normal emotional response to anything new, unexplored, uncharted.[2] It is a sense of tension, almost always tinged with fear, accompanied by certain physical changes that constitute the body's preparation for action: increased heart rate, rapid and shallow breathing, tightening of muscles, perspiration, often a trembling of the hands. In intensity it varies from the barely discernible to the extremely severe. In Chapter 7 I shall discuss anxiety and its countless disguises in greater detail, but for now it is sufficient to say that it constitutes the normal emotional response to new experience, and that hence it is inescapably associated with emergence from the incubator.

Unlike the butterfly, then, the young human is not only temporarily weak and inexperienced when he emerges from his social incubator. He is also anxious, and he is looking backward and inward at the same time. And to make a complicated matter still worse, the people who make up the framework of the social incubator seem to want their young one *not* to feel anxious, and to hope that he will not subject them and their setting to an objective appraisal; and if he tries for an objective look at himself they and their contemporaries too often tend to think of him, derogatorily, as selfish or sensitive or introspective. But at the same time he is expected—and he expects himself—to succeed scholastically or vocationally, socially, and perhaps athletically, to be determining at least the broad general outlines of his impending adult life, and to be taking his place in the world with increasing competence and independence. All in all, obviously, emergence from the incubator is something of an inauspicious start. It is not surprising, under these circumstances, that two or three or more years usually elapse before the young person is ready to come to grips with his own emergence, nor is it surprising that many fail, even then, to make the effort of growth. But despite adverse circumstances growth will occur if it is given the chance, even if the effort comes a little late.

Our inquiry will be focussed on the implications of the awareness with which one emerges into youth. I have already said that knowledge of oneself and of one's setting is a prerequisite to the achievement of maturity, and since much of what one is, in youth, depends upon one's earlier years, our attention will turn first to the social incubator within which those years were spent. Since it is a *social* incubator, we will be concerned with the people whose attitudes and beliefs, mistakes and triumphs, omissions and commissions gave it its form and content. Primarily, of course, the people involved are parents (or parent substitutes), and secondarily, they are society-at-large, the ambiguous and widespread abstraction of adults more like than unlike the parents who set the tone of the human world into which the new arrival is born. Of course, most young people know who their parents are, but frequently they do not really know much about their ultimate aims in life, their secret hopes and aspirations, their buried doubts and fears and guilts. Throughout the parental generation such things as these are generally subverbal, but the silence that surrounds them does nothing to minimize their power; and that power reaches its greatest strength in the unwitting parental effort to mold the child not in the parental image, but rather in an idealized parental image. In other words, children are often brought up to achieve the aims that have escaped their parents, to realize parental hopes and aspirations, to resolve parental doubts, to conquer parental fears, to escape parental guilts. This attempt to mold is commonly a major part of life in the incubator of childhood, and if the young person is to find his own identity he must know enough of his parents' identities to free himself from them.

The freedom I refer to here is sufficiently complex and important to warrant a brief digression. "Freeing" oneself from the identity of one's parents is not accomplished by moving to a new place physically distant from the parental home, or by cutting oneself off from the parents emotionally, or by denouncing and rejecting all the parents stand for. Rather it is a matter of identifying one's parents as the people they *think* they are, as the people they *seem* to be, and as the people they *really* are, and then discerning those elements of personality and aspects of belief they hope desperately to pass on to their children. Such an effort cannot fail to be accompanied by recognition, on the part of the child, of the poignancy of the parental effort—which means that the child, even as he is beginning to emancipate himself from the parental design, feels for his parents a new kind of love. In short, this freeing process is characterized by simultaneous feelings of warmth toward, and independence from, the parents. It is not a simple, quick, and relatively painless cutting of the silver cord at a single blow.

The idealized parental image from which the youth must free himself has a nobility that cannot be doubted, but its applicability to the contemporary world must be questioned. What would have been ideal when the parents of today's youth were young might well be burdensome, or even useless, today. A good beginning is to take a historical view of the world into which the parental generation was born and into which, at the beginning of their youth, *they* emerged. For a few of them, the years of incubation and the time of emergence occurred during a period of prolonged political stability and economic and technological growth. That era was rapidly approaching its cataclysmic end when they were young, but of course the end of an era can be seen clearly only in retrospect. To those who experienced it, it was a golden age. For generations, since the harnessing of steam and the democratization of government, civilized western man—at least in the economically favored social classes—looked forward with sublime confidence to an ever-increasing standard of living, an ever-expanding economy, an ever more solidly established political and social order, a permanent linear progression of technological advancement. The changes that inevitably occurred in the external world, from one generation to the next, were changes in degree only, not in kind. The status quo remained—it merely became bigger and better with each generation. What was good enough for grandfather was good enough for father, and that was good enough for son. In short, the world was by no means standing still, but its movement was orderly, predictable, and in a single direction. Business was big and ruthless, but it prospered and served the people. Government was small and noninterfering. Labor, for the most part, knew its place and presumably always would. This continent was considered physically inexhaustible and its people ambitious, energetic, hard-working, ingenious. In virtually every American family it was an article of faith that the man who did his work conscientiously would ascend the socio-economic ladder steadily, taking his wife and children with him, and that his children, in their time, would start where he left off, continuing the climb up a ladder that had no top.

The first World War marked the end of the era for Europe, but it did not have the same meaning here. Few

Americans were directly involved in the war; for the majority it was at most an interruption of the golden age. True, following the war there appeared the flappers, the speak-easies, the Charleston; but flappers were the exception, not the rule. They no more set the tone of their time than did the beatniks of the fifties. The tranquil era continued in this country until the boom ended with the bust: with the crash of the stock market and the ensuing great depression of the early thirties, the golden age closed with helpless bewilderment, anguish, futile rage, and the grinding, empty-bellied despair of massive unemployment. It was the beginning of a social and economic revolution, and in the short memories of many of those who survived it, it was the first time the world had not behaved itself in the old predictable way.

Only a few parents of today's youth were young themselves immediately before or during the upheaval, prepared during their incubation for life in the golden age of tranquillity. Most of the contemporary parental generation are younger and were brought up during the early years of the revolution, when everything was moving so rapidly that few people knew just what to prepare their children for. All of them, older and younger alike, have accommodated to the chaotic world that supervened after the crash, but for the majority it has been a makeshift accommodation. To their everlasting credit it must be said that, with some few exceptions, they knew their accommodation was precarious, and in their uncertainty about a new and unbelievable world they requested and accepted much help from many experts. Perhaps nowhere has this been more marked than in the area of child rearing. In the old days every mother knew how to raise her children—she did it the way *her* mother did it. But many of the mothers of today's youth knew they could not rely simply on old methods and precepts. So a generation of experts arose to tell them how to bring up their children—or, more accurately, two generations of experts. The first were the rigid-schedule people, the second the no-schedule, totally permissive people. And some mothers, Heaven help them, started with the first group and later graduated to the second.*

In many other areas the parental generation has displayed its uncertainties and insecurities by seeking out experts. Probably never before have there been so many professional experts—management consultants, sales consultants, expediters, industrial psychologists; psychoanalysts, psychiatrists, marriage counselors, child therapists; educational counselors, dietary counselors, religious counselors, public relations counselors. The point is worth stressing because it serves to illustrate the pervasiveness of uncertainty in the parental generation—an uncertainty to which few of its members give voice because few of them recognize its depth or extent, and of those few not many care to speak of it. Their actions, however, belie their silence: they do not comprehend this world. It has changed too much, too fast, in too many directions. Even so rudimentary a process as the teaching of simple arithmetic has become, for most of them, quite unrecognizable, with the introduction, of all things, of elements of Boolean algebra and calculus in elementary school. For these people the world is sick, abnormal, wrong, all wrong. But for youth, the same world is normal—chaotic, perhaps, but entirely normal. In their contemporary experience this is the way it has always been. And in regard to the world as it presently is, the greater objectivity is obviously youth's.

* Certainly not all experts in the field of child-care were characterized by the two extremes. Many were wiser than their colleagues at the two poles, but as is unfortunately usually the case the extremists were louder, more noticeable, and certainly more published. Consequently their extreme views colored, in a less than objective fashion, the whole field for too many years.

Without question, there have always been differences between successive generations—even the ancient Romans were sure that the younger generation was going to the dogs—but it is my own belief that seldom if ever before has there been a difference of such magnitude as that between today's youth and their parents. In many families in contemporary middle-class America the gulf seems to be virtually unbridgeable, as if no effective channels of communication exist between parent and child, as if each functions on unrelated wave lengths, as if the two generations speak different languages and rely on different basic assumptions. The extent of the present difference between the generations stems from the incredible amount of change to which the external world has been subjected in the past three or four decades, and although it makes psychological growth more difficult for today's youth, it also makes it more important. Until a generation or two ago, what was good enough for father was actually, in most details, good enough for son: but this simple equation is no longer valid.

So far I have been discussing an American-born middle-class parental generation. Many young people come from families that do not fit this description. Some grew up in tenements, some on impoverished dry-land farms, some in displaced persons camps in Europe, some in San Juan, Puerto Rico. Some grew up in Harlem or in Mobile or in the rural parishes of Louisiana, others on Ocean Avenue in Brooklyn in the building next door to the Temple, or on Jerome Avenue in the Bronx. And still others were brought up in the lap of material luxury in a Park Avenue triplex, or on the North Shore, or in Palm Beach. And I have not even mentioned Los Angeles, or upstate New York, or the German towns in Texas, or the Little Italys of New York or Boston, or the Japanese truck-gardens of the west coast. Some have parents who were divorced, or who died, or who are ill or alcoholic, or who failed to observe the formality of marriage. But regardless of individual instances, the essence of the matter remains: all have been brought up by parents who were brought up in a different time, a different world; and the great majority of those parents have had the best of intentions for their children.

But now back to the incubator: What kind of incubator could be built by well-meaning but confused people, prepared for life in a bygone age, bewildered by the world as it presently is, desperately desirous of rearing their children in such a way that they will be prepared to cope with still another world, one that is not yet even imaginable? Certainly it could not have been an ideal incubator. At best it provided the material needs of life, genuine love for the child, respect for him as a person, a functioning family setting for him to grow in, a basic education in the ways of the world as the parents saw it, and deep concern for his having to plot a course through an unforeseeable future alone, without parental help. This, of course, amounts to a very great deal, and those young people so fortunate as to have emerged from such a family setting will find little, if anything, new or unfamiliar in this book. They still have to find their own way, but at least they were brought up knowing it. Their childhood experience did not include answers to their present questions, but at least it allows them to believe that the questions are as they think they are. At the other extreme, at worst, the incubator provided the material needs of life—without them the child could not have survived to youth—but without love, without respect, without a functioning family setting, without the basic education, without concern for the child's future. Actually this extreme is theoretical rather than real: if an incubator as bad as this really existed, the few children surviving long enough to emerge into youth would be sick, probably even hopelessly sick. Of course, some few marginal and deviant families exist that fit this description, but it must be remembered that it is not only the family that makes up the incubator. The society in which the family exists contributes to the child's context too, and most children from such depriving households are able to find much that they need away from home, at school, on the street, with relatives.

The contexts from which most of today's youth have emerged lie somewhere between the two extremes. A typical example would be a setting providing the material needs and somewhat conditioned love (love was offered when the child was "good," in parental or societal terms, but was withdrawn, or its withdrawal was threatened, when he was "bad"). There was a fair measure of respect for the child as a person, but it extended mainly only to those aspects of him that were considered "respectable"—again, in parental or societal terms. The family setting in the typical example was functional, but sometimes largely on a superficial level: both parents were officially present most of the time but there may not have been much deep communication between them, and quite possibly, as a matter of fact, they really did not know each other very well. Parental disagreements may have been common, shared interests not so common. Mother took care of the house, the children, and her community responsibilities, and father took care of his job. A basic education in the ways of the world was provided, but the parental and societal view of the world and its demands, expectations, rewards, and punishments was perhaps so far out of touch with reality that much of the education was useless, and some of it downright dangerous. And finally, too often in the typical family the concern for the child's future took the form of doubts that he would be sensible enough and cooperative enough to live the kind of life his elders told him to live.

7244

Like the children of the grossly depriving family, those stemming from some variety of the typical household found much of what they needed outside the home. Given the normal human ingenuity that every child possesses, they ferreted out what they needed wherever they could. If a mother was too embarrassed to explain menstruation, her daughter found out about it from her friends or from her older sister. If a child was guilty about masturbation he finally found a book that said it was not so bad and he felt at least a little better. He probably kept quiet about many of his secret feelings of anger toward his parents, but he listened most attentively to any mildly rebellious schoolteacher who took it upon himself to say that parents are frequently fallible. If he believed himself to be abnormally moody or introspective or sensitive he was able to justify it, to some degree, after reading *The Catcher in the Rye*. All this, however, merely proves two points: first, the incubator is made up of more than one's parents; and second, the child in the incubator will make it as roomy and generous as he can. A third point remains to be made: if, on reaching the age of emergence, he found that the social incubator was not as generous as it should have been, despite his earlier unwitting efforts to broaden it, he had one more possibility. He could leave it, more or less on schedule, and move into another incubator setting, one that he hoped would provide him with the elements the first one lacked; and his ultimate emergence would then be merely postponed. And many young people have done just that. The "peer group" is frequently such a second incubator, and it can range all the way from the delinquent street gang to one's fellow-employees at the plant or office, or dormitory mates at college, or the girls at the YWCA. It can even be extended to marriage or graduate school or a more or less permanent job with a paternalistic corporation offering plenty of fringe-benefit security provisions.

But whatever the extent and composition of the incubator, once emergence has occurred the young person needs to examine it critically* and with as much objectivity as he can muster. Here he will very likely run into a difficulty of substantial proportions, because one of the things he probably learned while in the incubator was that parents should not be subjected to criticism. When parents were enlightened enough to avoid teaching this, grandparents, or the neighbors, or the schools and the church usually were not. However, as Socrates said, "The life which is unexamined is not worth living." We can paraphrase him and say, "The parents who are unexamined do not become persons who can be respected." Many young people hesitate to turn the cold light of critical objectivity upon their parents because they fear that as a result they will lose respect for them, but in practice exactly the opposite is true. To the child, parents are seen as two-dimensional figures. It is later, and then only if the youth exercises his new-found capacity of awareness, that he can see them three-dimensionally, as people, very human people with both strong points and shortcomings, very similar, as a matter of fact, to their nearly-grown children. *People* can be respected, if they are respectable, but parents are too likely only loved or feared. The rare parent who turns out, on examination, to be nonrespectable is one whose loss need occasion no mourning anyway.

Frequently, it must be said, parents themselves stand directly in the way of this development. Some of them fear the objective appraisal of their children, with its

* Throughout this book I use the words *critical* and *criticize* in their positive, constructive meanings, not in their censorious senses. According to the dictionary, *critical*, in this usage, means "Involving skillful judgment; exact; nicely judicious."

frequent but unnecessarily cruel sarcasm and impudence, and try to keep it from occurring. Youth, however, is capable of great compassion, and many a young one has observed his parents critically but with enough circumspection to spare them the pain of their needless fear. After all, it is by no means essential that the incubator know it is being subjected to scrutiny, and in view of the greater flexibility of youth it seems clear enough that in this regard the youthful generation is responsible for, as well as capable of, compassion.

Assuming that a young person finds it possible to peer objectively at his parents, there are certain fairly easily identified areas upon which he will need to focus. They have already been mentioned briefly. First, but certainly least important, is the question of love. Conditional it may have been, more easily lost by the child than gained, expressed more in punishment than in praise, perhaps petulant and martyred in flavor, but except in very rare instances it was there. In this regard it would be well to remember that anger is the other side of the two-faced coin—in childhood we feel anger only toward those whom, for whatever reason, we care about. The absence of love is not hate—it is indifference. True, many young people have one or two parents who have been less than adept at *showing* their love; perhaps they have had the puritanical notion that any display of emotion betrays weakness of character, perhaps they have had to concentrate almost exclusively on their own preoccupations, perhaps they were brought up to believe that the only adequate expression of love is the material gift, perhaps they have even told the child—or he has deduced—that he was the result of an unplanned and unwanted pregnancy. Nevertheless, it is a very rare and crippled adult who can live in the presence of a child, attending its needs, watching it grow, and still feel for it no love. In short, the question of parental love can be categorically answered: with exceptions that are exceedingly rare, parents love their children. *How* they express their love, however, is another question, and one worth a good deal of investigation. For otherwise it is all too easy for the child to follow in the parental footsteps, unthinking, unseeing, and to his own children apparently unloving.

The second area deserving of attention is parental respect for the child as a person and parental knowledge and understanding of him as a young and growing human organism, and here again a categorical answer is possible: that respect, knowledge, and understanding, when weighed, will be found wanting. Of course there are exceptions, but they are almost as rare as those in connection with parental love. A detailed examination of this one point will take up much of the bulk of this book; here I shall merely say that parents and society in general have certain very serious blind spots concerning young and growing human organisms. Once one has reached the beginning of youth, however, it is no longer a matter of importance whether his parents and their friends knew and understood the real *him*; for now he is capable of observing himself, as well as his context, and in retrospect he can become familiar with himself as he was as a child, as well as with himself now.

The third area of focus is as easy as it is important: what sort of functioning family setting was the youngster given to grow in? Easy, because the conscious memory can reconstruct it readily enough; important, because it provided the main structure or form of the incubator. How did the parents show their love for each other? To what extent did they feel respect for one another as persons? Did they agree or disagree or bicker or quarrel or fight? How much of each, and what about? How were their disagreements resolved? Or were they so circumspect about their feelings for each other that there is virtually no evidence to draw upon? What were their views, expressed or implied, toward sex, marriage, love, religion, politics, external appearances, education, material accomplishment, social status? What did—or do—they talk about with each other? What are their interests? Do they share any? How much, under what circumstances, and with whom do they drink? What are they living for? Do they know? Does their child know? How do they get along with friends, neighbors, relatives, the boss, salespeople? What do they spend their money for? What sort of house do they have, and what sort of community is it in? Are they satisfied with their place in society? Is the mother a good example of Woman, the father of Man? What is the state of their health? How do they behave at breakfast? What are their theories of child-rearing? What sort of background did each come from? What sort of reward and punishment did they mete out to their children? Any favoritism? Were they strict, lenient, or in-between? Did their children cry when it was time to go to school, or were they glad to get out of the house? Did they provide routine chores to do around the house? Were the children ever allowed to sit and read, or sit and think, or just sit? Do the parents read? How and where did they meet each other? What is the history of their life together? Where have they lived since marriage? Such a listing of questions could clearly go on forever. Obviously it is easier to sketch in the form of the incubator than it is to define its content, but even though it is easy, it needs to be done.

The fourth and fifth areas for perusal have to do with the *content* of the incubator, rather than with its form. The education the child was given by his parents in the ways of the world as they saw it, and their view of his future, provide ample indication of the sort of ideational material they inserted into the incubator. By "ideational," of course, I mean ideas, but more and stronger than that, I mean principles, values, beliefs, basic assumptions. All these are "ideas," but ideas placed on pedestals, supposedly beyond questioning or criticism. For example, parental ideas of religion, morality, politics, or material progress usually take on the color of "principles" or "values," and are not to be questioned, or even examined, by the child. But by our definition of youth as the period of life which begins with emergence from the incubator, and because of the awareness which characterizes that emergence, even parental principles become fit subjects for observation.

What *are* the principles taught by one's parents? Thrift, chastity, and Presbyterianism? Turn the other cheek, and maintain appearances? Speak softly, but carry a big stick? Be kind to animals, children, and women, but make a profit regardless of the cost? Succeed academically, and never mind marriage? Get married (to almost anybody promising), and never mind school? Keep the skirts clean, keep the nose clean, don't take any wooden nickels, don't go near the water, don't wash dirty linen in public, if you can't say something nice don't say anything, if you can't say something nice for heaven's sake say something? Be honest, don't steal, don't lie, think of others instead of yourself, do to others as you would have them do to you? The list is facetious, but the parentally dictated principle needs to be treated skeptically, sometimes even lightly. Its one unvarying characteristic is that is is *dictated*; and while dictation is not necessarily bad in itself, in this case it means that the principle in question is one that has meaning for the parent, that the well-intentioned parent is convinced it will have the same meaning for his child, that he gives it to the child ready-made and expects or at least hopes that he will accept it without quibbling. The trouble is that at best the principle has meaning for the parent because it was forged the hard way, from his own experience, in another time and place and under other circumstances. At worst, it really has no specific meaning for the parent, because he accepted it uncritically from his parents, and it is already two generations old. But even if it results from experience and has the deepest relevance for the parent, it can have none for the youth unless and until he gives it the test of his own experience, in his own time and place, under his own set of circumstances. I do not mean to imply, incidentally, that parents should have no principles, nor that they should not subject their children to the ones they do possess. After all, a child cannot build principles of his own, and if he is given none he will not survive his childhood. A youth, however, is capable of his own building, but before he can do it he needs a measure of freedom from parental principles, or at least permission to question them.

But we are not yet ready to discuss in detail the questioning of principles. For now it will suffice to point out that parental principles can be, and indeed need to be, examined objectively, for they contain at least by implication the clearest possible reflection of the parental views of the world, of the child as a person, and of his future position in the world. These parental views tend to be too simple, too black-or-white; but then the world of the parents' youth was, or they wish it had been, relatively simple. Parental views tend also to be contradictory, but the world now and the world then are contradictory. Parents, generally, would like to see their children as well-lubricated, well-built, smoothly functioning machines; the world of their children as a predictable, stable, and favorable setting for such machines; the child's future as that of the frictionless machine. Of course they really know better, but they cannot be blamed, in view of the upheavals they have had to survive, if they wish it otherwise.

Once the parental contributions to the incubator have been dealt with, the extraparental contributions can be discerned and dissected readily enough. Society-at-large, for the most part, serves a simple reinforcing function, backing up parental views and attitudes. However, it is well worth taking the time to identify those aspects of the incubator that the child found or made for himself. Their presence bears witness to the pleasant fact that even in childhood he was not entirely dependent and passive within the confines of a machine designed and operated by the vested authorities—even then he had some freedom, and he exercised it in his own behalf. Already, before emergence, he was to a significant degree self-made. Already the stage was being set for the greater effort to come, the objective view of himself, the delineation of his own identity and the discovery of his own way of life in this improbable and only world.

In summary, then, the retrospective observation of the incubator involves examination both of its form and its content. Its form is for the most part emotional in nature—the family was "warm and close" or "cold and distant." Parents were visibly loving and generous or apparently unloving and parsimonious; rigid, strict, and authoritarian or easygoing and permissive. Society-at-large was fairly tolerant, as in New York City, or highly ethnocentric, as in the Amish farm country. The content of the incubator, in contrast, is for the most part ideational in nature: parents display varying degrees of wisdom and knowledge; they range from rational to irrational. Very few American parents still believe the world is flat, but most of them "know" that all Russians are atheists. Only a few still believe that man's biological position is somewhere between animal and angel, but too many cling to the conviction that the sexual curiosity of the child is a nonhuman evil to be stamped out. Society-at-large has achieved an unprecedented level of technological knowledge, but it remains at a level of ignorance concerning the true nature of the human organism. But regardless of its rationality or irrationality, the child will learn the ideational content of the incubator. Its emotional form encourages him to learn or discourages the process, but learn he will, whatever is presented to him.

By now it will be obvious that I am convinced the child learns, during the incubator years, much that is inaccurate, unrealistic, irrational, downright wrong, and that much of the effort of his youth must be directed to learning what he needs to unlearn, and then to replacing it with material more in keeping with reality. It is clear, too, that this conviction of mine implies a rather sweeping denunciation of the ideational equipment of the parental generation, and indeed of society-at-large.[3] I shall not deny the implication, nor, having voiced it, will I attempt to defend myself. I shall rather conclude this chapter with a defense of the parental generation's possession of so unsatisfactory a body of knowledge to pass on to the young.

Once again the historical view is indicated. As I have said earlier, the great depression of the thirties marked the end of an era and the beginning of a social and economic revolution for which the members of the present parental generation were not prepared. And if that were not enough, they—and their children—are now involved in the beginning of another revolution, the second in a single generation. This one is, if anything, even greater than its predecessor in sweep and significance, for it is a technological, intellectual, and even moral revolution.[4] The parental generation, and their antecedents, made it inevitable by doing their work so well. Their work, their principal preoccupation, was technological mastery of the physical environment, and so proficient and persistent were they that now we can (a) destroy our physical environment utterly or (b) leave it for another. In other words, man's long-drawn-out effort to control his setting has reached a sort of zenith. Not that further technological developments will not or should not occur—obviously they must—but many of them will be in the nature of a mopping-up operation. We now have the technological means for ultimate control of our setting. We have very nearly reached the end of a line of intellectual pursuit and we —or more accurately, our children and grandchildren— will replace it with another. The central focus of our children's world will not be mastery of the physical environment; rather, it will be man's mastery of himself. We of the older generations have given our children the bomb, and it will be their responsibility to learn enough about man in general and themselves in particular to avoid lighting its fuse. So this is a tripartite revolution: technological, because a line of technological development has very nearly reached its end; intellectual, because the external focus of thought is rapidly becoming outmoded; and moral, because what was "right" when we needed to learn control of our world will not necessarily be "right" during the time when our children attempt to learn control of man.

So the poor parents have survived one revolution, to find themselves caught up in another only twenty-five years later. This is an incredible amount of change in a mere fragment of time. They cannot be expected to have kept up with it all, and in fact they deserve great praise for having survived it as well as they have. They have done their best, by and large, to teach their children what they know, and if what they know is no longer relevant or applicable, youth has the capacity, once emergence from the incubator has occurred, to learn on its own what *is* relevant. It has, too, feeling enough to respect the parental effort even if it was misguided—indeed, because it was misguided it was probably a greater effort than it would have been otherwise. Most likely the parents realized that the world as they knew it was becoming unrecognizable and so made an even greater attempt to teach youth *something, anything,* that might see them through the changing times—times their parents felt but could not know.

The test of youth will be in what *they* teach their children. This revolution is not only with us, it gives every indication of gaining more and more momentum, and its end is not yet in sight. We may well be facing many generations each of which will find it extremely difficult to communicate with its predecessors and its progeny. Perhaps this is the time to begin learning to live with such a radically new development.

****

It is his parents' fault that the youth is the way he is, but it is *his* fault if he stays that way. As he rectifies the teaching offered by his parents he will learn something about himself. If he learns enough about man in general he will come to know his own needs, his capacities, his limitations, his relationship to his changing world. In searching for his own identity he prepares himself for a mature life, and at the same time he carries forward the technological-intellectual-moral revolution that is the hallmark of his own moment in history. At one and the same time, his quest for the self is his own intimate personal affair and his destiny in fate.

REFERENCES

1. There are those who say that the specifically human capacity which distinguishes us from the rest of the animal kingdom is the gift of language, and others— distinguished among them is Ernst Cassirer—who say that the essence of the human being is the ability to form symbols. The first view is clearly a special example of the second, which has been stated most clearly by Cassirer: ". . . instead of defining man as an *animal rationale*, we should define him as an *animal symbolicum*. By so doing we can designate his specific difference . . ." (See Ernst Cassirer, *An Essay on Man*, New Haven, Yale University Press, 1944, p. 26). My own view is that symbol formation, and hence the development of language, derive of necessity from the quantitative sweep of man's awareness—both of himself and of his setting. The symbol is a necessary device for the categorization of human experience, a device that protects man from what, without it, would be an overwhelming flood of stimuli. Consequently, it seems to me that man's awareness, a function of the effective size of the human brain, constitutes the base upon which symbol formation in general, and the development of language in particular, rest; and that therefore it is his awareness, in the functional sphere, that distinguishes man from his nearest kin in the infrahuman world, just as the human brain distinguishes him in the structural or morphological sphere. In the development of this view I must acknowledge my debt to the existentialists (a concise view of whose psychology can be found in Rollo May, ed., *Existential Psychology*, New York, Random House, 1961); and to a Harvard group of investigators into the intricacies of the symbol and language (see J. S. Bruner, J. L. Goodnow, and G. A. Austin, *A Study of Thinking*, New York, John Wiley and Sons, 1956, and R. Brown, *Words and Things*, Glencoe, Illinois, The Free Press, 1958). See also

J. Church, *Language and the Discovery of Reality*, New York, Random House, 1961.

2. The ultimate source of anxiety has long been a matter of debate and of differences of opinion. Most personality theorists have considered anxiety to be a datum of pathology. For Freud anxiety constituted a flooding of the organism with an excess of stimuli with which the ego finds itself inadequate to deal. He assumed that the original experience of anxiety was associated with separation of the infant from the mother and saw the prototype of this experience to be the process of birth. Unlike Rank, however, he did not ascribe to the neonate the subjective feeling of anxiety, on the presumably legitimate grounds that the nervous system of the newborn infant is incapable of registering such an experience. That Freud considered anxiety a danger to the organism, if not explicitly pathological, seems assured by his teaching that "anxiety is the motive force behind repression." (See Ruth Munroe, *Schools of Psychoanalytic Thought*, New York, The Dryden Press, 1955, p. 441). Horney defined anxiety as ". . . the feeling a child has of being isolated and helpless in a potentially hostile world." (See Karen Horney, *Our Inner Conflicts*, New York, Norton, 1945, p. 41.) For Harry Stack Sullivan, according to Munroe, ". . . anxiety is . . . *always the fear of disapproval.*" (See Munroe, cited above, p. 405.) And in the account of Sullivanian theory given by Hall and Lindzey, "Anxiety is the experience of tension that results from real or imaginary threats to one's security . . . Severe anxiety is like a blow on the head; it conveys no information to the person but instead produces utter confusion and even amnesia." (See C. S. Hall and G. Lindzey, *Theories of Personality*, New York, John Wiley and Sons, 1957, p. 142.) But in their very next sentences these authors say, "Less severe forms of anxiety can be informative. In fact, Sullivan believes that anxiety is the first greatly educative influence in living." Here Sullivan, whose greatness was not reflected in the clarity of his articulations, appears to have anticipated the existential psychologists. Following a lead

first clearly voiced by Kierkegaard, they appear to accept anxiety as an inevitable and normal aspect of human life, and at least by implication treat it as the normal emotional response to a new experience. Rollo May, for example, writes, "Anxiety occurs at the point where some emerging potentiality or possibility faces the individual, some possibility of fulfilling his existence; but this very possibility involves the destroying of present security, which thereupon gives rise to the tendency to deny the new potentiality . . . If there were not some possibility opening up, some potentiality crying to be 'born,' we would not experience anxiety." (See Rollo May, "Contributions of Existential Psychotherapy," in R. May, E. Angel, and H. F. Ellenberger, eds., *Existence, a New Dimension in Psychiatry and Psychology,* New York, Basic Books, 1958, p. 52.) With regard to anxiety, as well as with regard to awareness, I claim kinship with the existential psychologists.

3. For other critiques of contemporary America relevant to the growth-struggles of youth, see D. Riesman, *The Lonely Crowd,* New Haven, Yale University Press, 1950; Erich Fromm, *Man for Himself,* New York, Rinehart and Co., 1947; W. H. Whyte, *The Organization Man,* New York, Simon and Schuster, 1956; Edgar Z. Friedenberg, *The Vanishing Adolescent,* Boston, Beacon Press, 1959; and Paul Goodman, *Growing up Absurd,* New York, Random House, 1960.

4. For a discussion of what he calls the "Revolution of Modernity" see G. Frankel, *The Case for Modern Man,* New York, Harper and Brothers, 1955.

2

The Biological Foundation

Our youth has a double heritage. In terms of technological triumph and material plenty, American youth has inherited an accomplishment of vast magnitude; and in terms of self-knowledge and its extension, comprehension of man in general, it has inherited a challenge of equal magnitude. It has been called the generation without a cause, and possibly the old causes *have* been worked and reworked and overworked until their meaning is thin, but here is a new cause whose significance will be whatever youth gives it. Of course the idea that one can come to know oneself, and hence to know man in general, is not a new one. Doubtless it has been realized by a few individuals in every generation, in every culture, since the origin of the species. But its systematization by means of the scientific approach was conceived by Freud only a little more than a half century ago, and beneath the sound and turmoil of the revolutionary changes of recent decades it has pursued its quiet gestational course. Not until now has the idea grown enough in the womb, so to speak, for its delivery to a substantial percentage of a waiting and ready generation. In other words, not until very recently has social science known enough to offer a primitive systematic approach to the search for individual identity, and not until very recently has the wheel of history in its turning reached a generation whose fate it is to make that search.

As searchers after identity contemporary youths are pioneers, and as teachers of the systematic way of the search we social scientists are beginners. We know enough for a beginning, but our body of knowledge is riddled with gaps and guesses, and we are not always in agreement with each other. For example, in the pages to follow there are passages that will elicit objection, disagreement, and debate from some of my colleagues. I will set forth only what I personally believe to be valid, rounded out here and there with guesses, educated and otherwise, but what I have to say is far from gospel. I am not of the youthful generation—I am on the outside looking in, as are my colleagues. None of us can do more than offer youth a few pointers. In their own time they will teach their children what we do not yet know.

As the young person freshly out of the incubator begins his search for his own identity he will frequently be frightened by the shakiness of his legs and the immaturity of his judgment, and in his fear he will run back to his parental home. This is a wise action, and one hopes a sufficiently receptive family exists to make the occasional return useful. Such a return to the incubator is sometimes called "regression," a word that has unfortunate psychiatric connotations, but for the young person who is working toward his own sense of identity the return is only temporary and partial. It is not a "bad" sign—it is simply an indication that a little more has been bitten off than can readily be chewed, or that a more than usually painful foray into the world has been attempted, not entirely successfully, which needs to be followed by a strategic retreat in order to regroup forces and lick fresh wounds. Once the chewing is done, the forces regrouped, the wounds healed, the young one will sally forth again in another attempt. As time passes and experience accumulates he will notice that his retreats to the incubator are fewer and farther between and shorter lived. If his family is not sufficiently receptive for this kind of temporary retreat he will find a substitute that does offer him a welcome, even if it is nothing more than his own room with the door closed and the radio on to obscure the sound of his crying. Such a pattern of growth is characteristic of nearly all young animals: puppies typically make ever-longer exploratory trips away from the litter, only to run back fast if a sudden gust of wind lifts a fearsome dry leaf a few feet away. And even half-grown robins, days out of the nest and accomplished worm-diggers, once in a while pester the oldsters for parent-dug worms.*

Another early difficulty associated with the search for identity, and one that sometimes demonstrates nagging persistence, is a feeling of confusion between what one *really* is and what one is *supposed* to be. The preceding paragraph illustrates the point that the young human *is* an inexperienced, uncertain, frequently frightened person. Very likely he has been taught that he is *supposed* to be, at seventeen or eighteen or nineteen, poised, relaxed, comfortable, in command of himself, mature, adult. But the preceding paragraph illustrates another point: that he is really a young animal, although he has probably been taught that man is better

* I am clinging tenaciously to my analogies and comparisons featuring butterflies, puppies, and robins, despite the criticism of some of my valued friends. I am not taking this stand out of stubbornness, but rather because I am convinced that the human late adolescent is a younger and less biologically mature organism than society in general likes to believe. It is interesting to note that very few youthful readers of earlier versions of the manuscript objected to such comparisons. The objections have come almost exclusively from adults.

than, "higher" than, animals. Not too long ago, throughout the western world, man's biological origins were denied on a widespread and "official" basis, and vestiges of that denial persist to this day—despite Darwin, the Scopes trial, and the passing of a century.

Man *is* an animal, the youth is a young human animal, and no better foundation can be laid for the quest for one's own identity than a biological foundation. Consequently I shall attempt to sketch in, as succinctly as is feasible, an outline of human biological growth. Of course man is a *social* animal, so no outline of biological growth alone can do justice to the whole picture; but biology is basic to culture, and we cannot adequately understand the cultural or social forces to which we are subject without knowing something of the underlying biological framework. So the biological basis first, and cultural influences later.[1]

Among animals man is obviously unique, and the anatomical feature responsible for his uniqueness is his brain. In comparison with our nearest relatives, the great apes, we have very big brains, in the sense that they are commodious. They hold more; consequently we know more. The human eye is probably no better than the chimpanzee's—both we and they can see the stars—but no chimpanzee ever thought of building a telescope. Because of the capacity of the human brain we can make more connections or associations than any other species. We see the stars and we know they are so distant we cannot make them out well. But we also know about lenses: we know that the right juxtaposition of lenses brings a distant view closer. So we connect stars and lenses, two very different kinds of objects, and create the telescope to bring the stars closer. Perhaps this is merely a difference of degree between us and the great apes. An ape confronted with a bunch of bananas too high to reach, and a long pole, connects bananas, distance, and pole; after a few tries he manages to use the pole to knock down the bananas. But it is at least a large difference of degree: light rays are a much less tangible reaching instrument than a pole, and the ape's reward for his mental work is a full stomach, whereas ours is partial satisfaction of our curiosity.

But a qualitative difference exists too, a difference of *kind*: so far as can be determined, it is the human brain and the human brain only that is capable of self-awareness. James Thurber illustrates the point with his quip, "The noblest study of mankind is Man, says Man." [2] Because of this capacity for self-awareness the human animal can "see" itself as well as its setting. We can connect the past self with the present self, and even speculate about the future self. We can associate the effects of our actions with the self that does the acting —an accomplishment beyond the reach of my dog, who occasionally sees her own reflection in the window at night and bristles and growls at it. In contrast, my one-year-old daughter recognizes her image in the mirror, laughs and talks to it, allows it to be referred to with her name, tries to lean forward to kiss it. Self-awareness, however, is not limited to self-loving. It is also the basis for responsibility, another characteristically human accomplishment. For example, it appears to be only the human father who knows that an action of his own was involved in the conception of his children.*

In other words, that part of our biological base that makes us specifically human is the part having to do with self-awareness. If one is to pursue one's ability for

* It is possible that this is a special and still evolutionarily quite new application of self-awareness. For example, Eugene Burdick says of the Australian aborigine, "Many aborigines have not yet made the association between sexual intercourse and conception. When a woman realizes she is pregnant she instantly associates the condition with something in the immediate surroundings: a tree, a hill, a cloud, a rock. A whirlwind, a rolling cloud of dust, is thought to be especially virile and these women will flee in terror at the sight of one." E. Burdick, "The Invisible Aborigine," *Harper's*, 233:1336, Sept., 1961, p. 76.

self-awareness to its goal—the sense of personal identity
—it will help to have some familiarity with its origins.

Growth of self-awareness appears to run parallel to
growth and maturation of the physical body, and five
fairly distinct steps in the course of growth can be discerned. Boundaries between the steps are fluid, rather
than sharply fixed; the steps tend to overlap; if a given
step cannot be dealt with satisfactorily it may crop up
later, at a more propitious time; ages marking the end
of one step and the beginning of the next are subject to
considerable individual variation; and finally, any developmental scheme is, inevitably, an oversimplification
for purposes of clarity, a cutting-and-drying of issues
that are, in life, neither cut nor dry. Bearing these pre-
cautions in mind, let us identify the five steps.[3]

From soon after birth until he is about two and a half
the child's self-awareness is limited mainly to the *physical* sphere. The baby first discovers his body and then
slowly acquires mastery of its functions. At first he
finds his mouth, his hands and feet and arms and legs,
his belly, his hair, his ears and nose and eyes and genitals. He finds he can kick and wave his arms and wiggle
his fingers and yell, he learns to turn over in his crib,
to turn back again, to sit up, to crawl, to stand, to walk,
to run, to jump and skip and play hopscotch. He learns to
eat with his fingers and then with a spoon, he learns
to control bowel and bladder and to use with proficiency
the potty-seat. He falls occasionally and cuts his lip,
he puts pebbles in his nose and ears, he explores his own
anatomy and that of his playmates if he has the chance,
sometimes he absent-mindedly wets his pants. In short,
with regard to himself this is a period of discovery,
exploration, and mastery of his own body. Obviously
the child in this first or physical stage of development
is doing many other things too—he is certainly discovering and exploring his environment—but interest here
needs to center on the question of self-awareness.

From two and a half to about five the child's self-awareness is concentrated primarily on *emotional* matters. Not that he displayed no feelings earlier—most parents would say he had displayed more than enough. But now he begins to discover his feelings in the sense that he learns names for them; he begins to learn how they affect others; he begins to learn the rudiments of controlling them. As in the physical stage of development, so now: the course of growth is not always smooth. The emotional equivalent of the bean in the nose is probably the deliberate temper tantrum. Each represents a worthy enough experiment, but neither much benefits the young experimenter. (But then most of our learning, perhaps all of it, is learning by experiment, by trial and occasional error.) As this second period of growth approaches its close the new feeling of *guilt* becomes established, but this is a cultural, rather than a biological, development.*

At about five the focus of self-awareness again undergoes a change. By this time the child is physically grown enough to spend a substantial amount of time away from home, in the company of his contemporaries, and in terms of self-awareness this is the *social* stage. From now until the approach of puberty the child will be engaged in the discovery, exploration, and mastery of himself as a *social* being. He will discover within himself the rudiments of compassion and of assertiveness, of cooperation and competition. He will have friends and enemies, and he will learn techniques for dealing effectively with both. Characteristic of this social stage of development are the secret societies of childhood, the groups and clubs whose inner workings are not shared with adults. It is of interest to know that childhood has a culture all its own, one within which the

---

* My contention that guilt is primarily a culturally determined feeling is further illustration of my argumentative position set forth under References, no. 1, p. 41.

social attributes can be developed without too much adult interference, one that has an ancient and honorable lineage. Many of the games of contemporary children have survived essentially unchanged since at least the day of ancient Rome. Apparently it has never been particularly easy to grow up.

With the advent of puberty, self-awareness turns obviously enough to sex, ushering in the *sexual* stage of development. Now the young person—no longer can we refer to him as a child—discovers himself to be a sexual being and once again enters the familiar sequence of discovery, experimentation, and mastery. This time experimentation may take the form mainly of night dreams and day dreams for a period of two or three years, and mastery in the fullest sense will have to be postponed until still later. But the discovery phase is visible and very much present. No young adolescent can fail to heed the powerful physical changes of puberty that alter the shape and appearance of the body itself.[4]

Following the dramatic occurrence of puberty, at about fifteen or sixteen, comes the fifth and last stage in the development of self-awareness, the cognitive stage. In this stage occurs the emergence from the incubator; it is the stage youth is still in. *Cognitive* simply means *knowing*: once the adolescent enters the cognitive stage of development he is capable of knowing himself. Now he "discovers" in himself facets with which previously he had been unfamiliar: moodiness, shyness, aggression, a great capacity for daydreaming; a widespread fear of people, perhaps, or rankling resentment toward authorities; anxiety in any of its countless forms; and probably above all else, a capacity for criticism of self and of others, combined with introspection, preoccupation, touchy sensitivity, and a painful degree of self-consciousness. Experimentation in this stage of growth arises from the new ability to observe and to criticize. The youth who feels himself to be socially clumsy and inept, who criticizes himself for his social shortcomings, frequently chooses a suave acquaintance as a model and experimentally tries to be like him. A girl may decide she is unduly prudish and naive and so she experiments, for a time, with the role of the "loose" (but cautious and scared) woman. Experimentation in this stage of growth also involves opinions, beliefs, convictions. Experimental questioning and criticizing of parental, social, and institutional policies is commonplace—for example, how many at this age agree wholeheartedly with parental views of religion, social views of morality, the grading system at school, the promotion policy at the place of work? Much experimenting occurs in the area of independence, with an occasional rapid retreat from the end of a long and shaky limb. And of course, following all this discovery and experimentation, there will come, in time, a welcome degree of mastery.

Very briefly, then, these are the biological stages through which the young human passes in the development of his capacity for self-awareness. Each stage—physical, emotional, social, sexual, and cognitive—is characterized by specific content, and in each it is possible to see the sequence of discovery, experimentation, and mastery. Each stage occurs when, physically and mentally, the child is ready for it. When bones, muscles, and nervous system are sufficiently developed, the baby learns to walk. When speech and the ability to observe his feelings are sufficiently developed the three-year-old learns to distinguish between love and hate. When he has grown still more, both physically and mentally, the child of six is capable of dealing socially with his contemporaries. When glands mature, puberty occurs. And finally, when growth in both body and mind is essentially complete, "knowing" becomes possible.

There is an air of inevitability about this biological sequence of growth—that which is dictated by nature occurs, more or less on schedule, regardless of external circumstances—but what happens to it after it occurs is subject to very wide variation. But this, too, is in the biological nature of man. A grown-up bird discovers her nest-building ability, and immediately, without the need for experimentation, builds a perfectly adequate nest. Because she has what was formerly called an *instinct*, a built-in, biologically inherited pattern for a particular kind of activity, she does not have to learn how to build a nest; as soon as she is mature enough to lay eggs she *knows* how to build it. Her "instinct," * in other words, saves her the time-consuming trouble of learning, but it also drastically limits what she can do. A robin can only build a robin's nest and an oriole an oriole's nest. In human beings, by contrast, "instincts" are much less important and powerful. We can probably say that the baby's discovery of his body is "instinctual," but then to some degree he has to *learn* what to do with it. The toddler's discovery of his feelings is probably "instinctual," but then, and to a greater degree, he has to learn how to control them. And so on through the five biological stages: the phase of discovery in each may be "instinctual," but with each successive stage the phase of experimentation becomes more a matter of learning. Clearly this makes for slow growth—it may have a lot to do with the fact that the human animal requires about a fourth of its lifetime to achieve maturity—but it also makes for a much greater degree of freedom, of variation. A Texas housewife could learn to build as good an igloo as an Eskimo hunter, and the two conceivably could learn to discuss architecture with each other in, say, Finnish.

But there is another consequence of the biological human need and ability to learn, as opposed to the other-animal reliance on "instinct." Where there is

---

* I enclose the word *instinct* in quotation marks to indicate its changing connotations.

learning, there is also teaching, and the former is largely dependent upon the latter. A baby cottontail rabbit born into a society of American rabbits will grow up to be very similar in his behavior to one born into a society of Siberian rabbits; but a human baby born into a society of Welshmen will grow up to be very different indeed in his behavior from one born into a society of Polynesians. In short, the cultural setting into which the human being is born is of extreme importance to the subsequent development of his sense of identity, simply because so much of that development results from experimentation, from learning—a process that is inevitably accompanied by teaching. Ideally teaching encourages learning, but unfortunately it can also discourage, inhibit, or even subvert it.

To sum up this chapter, the youth is a young human animal who has passed through four stages of development of his biologically given capacity for self-awareness and is in the fifth. He has discovered in himself his body, his feelings, his social propensities, his sexuality, his capacity for knowledge. He has experimented with each—which is to say he has learned about each—as far as he could, under his particular set of culturally dictated circumstances. Where learning has been encouraged, or at least tolerated, he has achieved a measure of mastery. Where it has been discouraged or blocked, mastery has not been possible. Being human, he *is* dependent upon his cultural setting for a matrix within which his experimentation and learning occur. And finally, being human, he *is* vulnerable to faulty teaching. It is worth repeating that he is tremendously dependent upon the teaching context within which he has done his learning—he cannot simply rely on *"instinct"*—but now that he has reached the cognitive stage he is mature enough for his dependence on that context to be reduced. Now he can choose a context that suits him, at least within limits, rather than make do with one that was presented to him through no choice of his own. For now he is aware of what he really *is*.

What he is *supposed* to be is something else again. This depends on the convictions of the social incubator he was born into, and here the widest variation occurs. What a seventeen-year-old Bushman is supposed to be, and what a seventeen-year-old upper-middle-class Protestant American is supposed to be, are literally worlds apart. Yet both are seventeen-year-old human males who have traversed the same biological growth sequence. I do not wish to imply that whatever one is *supposed* to be, in contrast to what one really *is*, is necessarily bad: the Bushman is supposed to be a competent hunter, and indeed he had better be, or he won't eat. The American is supposed to be capable of understanding a highly complicated social-economic-technological world, and if he can't he won't eat either. Both are capable, however, of distinguishing between the reality and the "supposed-to-be" (although the American's chances of doing so are very much better than the Bushman's).* It is one thing to know one is supposed

---

* The American youth's chances of distinguishing between reality and the "supposed-to-be" are better than the Bushman's because the American has more freedom to make the distinction. It seems logical to assume that the more widely the cognitive stage of development is recognized in a society, the greater the opportunity, the greater the freedom for the young to make this sort of distinction. In most societies—among them, doubtless, that of the Bushmen—this stage is not recognized, and in consequence youth has very little freedom to question, to explore, to be critical of the social order. In our society the cognitive stage is beginning to be recognized, although recognition is much more implicit than explicit, so our youth have what might be termed a moderate degree of such freedom. It should be pointed out, too, that the growth characteristic of the cognitive stage is something of a luxury. Young people cannot afford it if they must bend all their efforts toward fending off starvation or defending themselves from enemy tribes. In all probability such freedom, and consequently such growth, can occur only in societies in which there is a reasonably high standard of living coupled with a reasonably high level of physical security.

to be a good hunter, and that it requires one's best efforts to approach that level of competency; it is another thing to believe that one was born to be a *perfect* hunter, and that anything less reflects on the essence of one's being. Similarly, it is one thing to know that one is supposed to be charitable, altruistic, loving, and Christian, and that it requires one's best efforts to approach *that* level of competency; it is quite another thing to believe that these attributes were allegedly born into you, that everyone else demonstrates them to perfection, that you and you alone fall short of the ideal. In other words, much of what one is supposed to be makes very good sense, but it may well be different from what one in fact *is*. And some of it, of course, makes no sense at all, even though almost everyone seems to think it does.

The next step, then, must be to examine what youth is supposed to be, to determine the sensible suppositions and those which are not so sensible, to contrast both with what the young human being really is. Perhaps the best route to this goal lies in an examination of the cultural context within which youth has grown, and more specifically, in an investigation of the views held by that context with regard to each of the five biological steps mentioned in this chapter. This effort involves another look at the social incubator, but a look in greater detail, in sharper focus. With luck it will illuminate the conflicts young people encounter between their learning and their teaching, between what they are and what they are supposed to be.

REFERENCES

1. My attempt to distinguish between *biology* and *culture* will bring forth heartfelt objections from many of my colleagues in the social sciences. It has probably never been particularly fashionable to delve too deeply into man's biological nature, since he prefers to see himself as in some way superior to the rest of the animal kingdom, and most of the criticism leveled at Darwin stemmed from the fact that he demonstrated with implacable logic that man was, indeed, part and parcel thereof. Early efforts by social science to define man's nature were one-sidedly *cultural*: they led to the inescapable dead end of the supraordinate society, to the illogical conclusion that society makes the individual, that the state is greater, by definition, than the sum of its citizens. As the lack of logic of this view became evident corrective measures set in; but perhaps out of caution they failed to go to the opposite extreme that would say, in effect, that biology is all, culture counts for little if anything.

    At about the same time biologists in the infrahuman field were discovering more "cultural" factors than they had previously recognized—for example, the notion of "instinct" was found to be much less clear-cut than they had supposed. It was discovered, for instance, that a bird does not sing its species-specific song unless it has had the opportunity to hear it sung by older birds during a particular span of its early days, so it could no longer be said that the song of a bird is purely instinctual. Obviously, there is also some element of *learning* involved, and this means there must be a cultural context within which it occurs. It is of course entirely clear that in infrahuman species such learning involves very little flexibility—a robin, for example, can learn the song of the robins, but he cannot learn the song of the chickadees. Nevertheless the discovery that learning in these species coexists with instinct was a discovery of very great magnitude.

This discovery was seized upon by the social scientists, who may understandably have been somewhat embarrassed about elevating culture to such an insupportable height, and they now tend to utilize it in defense of their position that no distinction can be made between the biological and the cultural in the human sphere since, in their view, the distinction can no longer be made in the infrahuman. Having overemphasized the cultural aspects of man, and continuing to underemphasize the biological, they are currently taking refuge in the contention that the two cannot and must not be distinguished. In my view this is an untenable position, and I suspect that it illuminates the fact that most social scientists lack training in the biological sciences.

Without question, the human animal cannot be understood in terms of his biology alone, nor can he be understood in terms of his acculturation alone. We have begun to find that the same is true also of the robin, the dog, probably even of the earthworm and the amoeba. But this is not the same as saying that the two coexisting aspects cannot be examined separately as well as together in their harmoniously functioning interdependence. After all, in a functioning automobile it requires the cooperative coexistence of carburetor and gasoline for a supply of usable fuel, but no one would deny that on occasion the carburetor needs to be examined separately, and that on other occasions the gasoline needs to be analyzed. I insist that the same holds true for man—he functions only in a cultural field, he can become truly human only in a human cultural context, but he is at the same time a biological entity. He can be studied for his *cultural* verities, and he can also be studied for his *biological* verities. He has both. If, to many of my colleagues, my view appears to be mine alone, if not downright autistic, perhaps it is because by bent, by experience, and by practice I am a biologist and physician first, a psychiatrist second, and a social scientist third.

2. James Thurber, "The Human Being and the Dinosaur," in *Further Fables for our Times*, New York, Simon and Schuster, 1956, p. 69.

3. Despite the usually cautious approach to such a schematization as my five developmental steps, and despite the disclaimers as to fluidity of boundary lines, overlapping of steps, and the like, these divisions, chronologically speaking, have been made by others viewing the young organism from different angles. See E. Erikson, *op. cit.*, Reference no. 7, Introduction; L. J. Stone and J. Church, *Childhood and Adolescence*, New York, Random House, 1957; B. Inhelder and J. Piaget, *The Growth of Logical Thinking*, New York, Basic Books, 1958. The table on the next page shows the parallels.

4. For a thoroughly detailed description of the years of growth see L. J. Stone and J. Church, *op. cit.*

Age	My developmental steps	Freud	Erikson	Stone & Church	Inhelder & Piaget
1	Physical	Pre-genital	Trust vs. Mistrust	Infancy	Sensory-motor period
2			Autonomy vs. Shame & Doubt	Toddlerhood	
3 4 5	Emotional	Oedipal	Initiative vs. Guilt	Preschool	
6 7 8 9	Social	Latency	Industry vs. Inferiority	School	Preoperational thinking
10 11					Concrete operational thinking
12 13 14	Sexual	Puberty & Adolescence	Identity vs. role diffusion	Puberty	
15 16 17 18	Cognitive	Young Adulthood		Adolescence	Formal thinking

3

The Cultural Matrix

Experimentation takes place in laboratories, and we Americans are accustomed to believe that the better the laboratory, the better the experiment. We are also accustomed to believe that the quality of the laboratory depends upon the quality of its equipment—the more modern the instruments, the more controlled the climate, the more voltage available, the more chrome finish, the better the laboratory. Certainly the experimenter is aided by adequate equipment, but his success depends more upon another factor. Edison's laboratory, in his early years, was ill-equipped, and the Wright Brothers' was worse, and Newton's, according to legend, was nothing more than a place to sit beneath an apple tree. Yet from these primitive laboratories came results of incalculable importance. In contrast, from some of our magnificent and even opulent modern laboratories we have obtained tooth paste with colored stripes and a delicious taste, enriched bread with no taste at all, and "clean" hydrogen bombs. To discover why a laboratory produces what it produces, we must turn our backs on its equipment and ask the crucial question, "Who's in charge here?" In Edison's laboratory, Edison was in charge, and the Wrights managed their own barn, and

Newton was alone with his thoughts under the tree. But the tooth paste laboratory is directed by a man who believes that tooth paste should be measured by its salability, the bread laboratory by a man who believes that bread requires vitamins more than flavor, and the nuclear laboratory by a man who believes that the best defense is an impossible offense.

I seem to have made "laboratory" synonymous with "incubator," and although the metaphors are mixed, technological, and clumsy they at least illustrate two important aspects of human growth: it takes place in the protective setting of a social structure, the "incubator," and it consists in large part of experimentation in a "laboratory." It is our next task to examine the laboratory, to ask "Who's in charge here?" and "What does he believe?" in order to determine the quality of the experimentation that occurs as growth proceeds.

Obviously the setting for experimentation is in charge of parents in particular and society in general, and the question, "What do they believe?" is much too big and varied to be answered in any narrowly specific way. However, a generalization can be drawn, and so long as it is treated as a generalization, as a great overriding theme subject to innumerble variations, it can do no harm. The character of our American cultural body of belief is partly derived from the Protestant ethic, with its undertones of Puritanism and Calvinism, transplanted from an old and crowded Europe to the new and wide-open continent of North America. Certainly we have huge minorities that are not Protestant, others that are not Christian, still others not of European origin, and the continent is no longer so new nor so boundless; and certainly our body of belief adheres less to the Protestant ethic than it did a generation or two ago. Nevertheless, despite migrations, the bubbling of the melting pot, the vast increase and diversification in population, and the passage of years, the Protestant ethic remains at the base of our "official" body of belief.

As I am using it here, the word *ethic* means an outlook or view concerning the essential nature of man. Such a view is made up of assumptions that are not often voiced and still less often questioned or tested, assumptions that are accepted blindly and passively because they have been handed down from generation to generation for a very long time and because they had their origins in an unimpeachable, if no longer remembered, authority. Usually such assumptions undergo a slow evolutionary process of misinterpretation during the centuries of transmission, and it is at least conceivable that in the course of so much time the accrual of new knowledge renders questionable the validity of the original assumptions. The origins of the Protestant view of man go back at least as far as the rabbinical teaching that antedated Christ, and whether or not it was realistic then, there seems very little reason to believe that it has improved with age. Obviously, too, it has long since lost its relationship to religion. It has become thoroughly secularized: that is, it has been taken from its earlier religious context and placed in worldly service. This is not an unusual transformation, of course. More than one idea, at first religious in nature, has been taken over for worldly purposes—the commercialization of Christmas is a case in point, and the status-seeking function of the bar mitzvah or the wedding another. In short, in this discussion of what is commonly called the Protestant ethic I am not attacking religion or the churches, but rather a view of man that has been removed from a religious context and modified, shaped, molded, and warped to worldly uses.

The Protestant view of the nature of man, as it seems most commonly to exist in contemporary society, has it that man is inevitably a sinner, that his life on this earth will be at best a compromise between his innately evil nature and his aspirations for good, and that if he aspires sufficiently he will find rest—presumably from the conflict of the compromise—in the life hereafter. His salvation, meaning the triumph of his aspiration for good over his evil nature, is held to be his own personal responsibility rather than that of a priest or of society; and salvation involves, in one way or another, self-sacrifice or self-renunciation. In other language, this view of man holds that he is born imperfect and his life on earth will be at best an unending and ultimately futile struggle against inborn imperfection, but that if he struggles enough and denies himself enough he will have his reward in eternity.

Part of the basis for this view has been called ". . . a preposterous piece of medieval sophistry" [1] but the notion that man is somehow a strangely imperfect creature is of course understandable enough in the light of history. Until Darwin upset the intellectual applecart we did not know that man was just another animal, albeit a pretty complicated one. We considered him, instead, to stand somewhere between animal and angel, better than the former, not as good as the latter. This concept is a very old one and probably had its origins in the mists of prehistory. We can hardly expect it to have died in the mere century since Darwin. Even Freud, for all his sophistication and his renunciation of organized religion, reflected precisely this view; and he was hardly Christian, much less Protestant. He taught that man consists of the Id (dark, unconscious, utterly unprincipled, animal-like) and the Superego (harsh, demanding, the ultimate source of social rules and regulations). Between them stands the Ego, that relatively weak and powerless agent whose responsibility it is to effect the unending and futile compromise between evil and good.

This is not only a pessimistic view of the nature of man, it is also a harsh one. The individual who accepts it sentences himself, in effect, to a life on earth whose only reward is struggle for its own sake. And since the opposite of struggle is pleasure, any sign of pleasure indicates an absence of struggle. Struggle or work then becomes virtuous, and pleasure, or any other form of nonwork, becomes a vice. In this regard it is of interest that in India, where a different ethic prevails, surprise is voiced that we in the west provide no time in the day for reflection. But of course to us quiet reflection means an absence of work; therefore it is to be avoided. We would be likely to label reflection with the disparaging word idleness. If pleasure is a vice, certainly the most vicious pleasure is that of the flesh. Here we are probably treading on very old ground again—it seems obvious that carnal pleasures are animal pleasures, and if we are to deny the animal in us, we must forego the animal pleasures.

Another consequence of this view of man involves the emotions. In general, the Protestant view holds that they are not to be expressed. Anger, of course, is popularly considered basically unchristian. We are to love our neighbor, to turn the other cheek. But love, too, is suspect: if it is not directly related to sex, which is one of the animal pleasures, it is at least a sign of weakness, and strength is necessary if one is to struggle. And anxiety suggests that the struggle for compromise is not going well, so it too must be avoided.

In summary, then, the Protestant view appears to be that man is basically imperfect, that he must struggle always against his imperfections and for the good that cannot be attained but only aspired to, and that any sign of surrender to the bad or animal in him is disastrous, as is any sign of weakness in the lifelong struggle. It is of course obvious that this secularized Protestant view, as it is currently held, is a perversion of the teaching of Christ. He did not deny His feelings—it is difficult in the extreme to imagine Him throwing the moneylenders from the temple without wrath; certainly

He knew love; and without any question He felt anxiety in Gethsemane.*

It is interesting to examine the world view held by our society in the light of the Protestant ethic. Because its view of man is so harsh and temporally unrewarding the individual is seen as foredoomed to a life devoid of internal accomplishment; so he turns instead to external accomplishment. Because the continent was at first so challenging, so rich, and so empty, except for a few benighted Indians who were not Christian, it was easy and understandable to turn to exploitation of the land for a sense of external accomplishment. Consequently there arose even in the most righteous of the Believers the ruthless laissez-faire attitude toward the physical environment that is still giving us no end of trouble. More recently, as exploitation of the continent has become progressively less possible, exploitation of the social setting has taken its place; and where a few generations ago a young man made his mark by carving an empire out of the land, he now achieves the same end by making his impression on people, if possible on Madison Avenue, or in Beverly Hills, or in Grosse Pointe. In other words, although the view of man is characterized by a most stringent conscience, the view of what he may do with—or to—his external world has attached to it almost no conscience at all.†

* I am much indebted to Howard Howson, Professor Emeritus of Religion, Vassar College, for clarification of my views concerning the Protestant ethic.

† Note, for example, the incredible and really almost systematic way in which we are still violating our land. We pollute our rivers and air, we surround our cities with junk yards and the most evil of "eating" establishments. We fill the landscape with signs, we let the centers of our cities fester and die in urban blight. Power lines, superhighways, and dams are laid out with no regard for natural beauty, the public domain is given away for private exploitation, and always the excuse has something to do with "Free Enterprise." So far as I know, we are unique among nations in our apparent dedication to fouling our own nest as irreparably as possible.

It is at this point that the worldly usefulness of such a view of the nature of man becomes evident. If man's aim is to conquer his physical environment, he will go at it more avidly if he is convinced that he has no opportunity to better his inner self instead. If he is convinced of his own essential imperfection, he cannot object too strenuously to a lifetime's work tending a machine. If work is virtuous in and of itself he will be a compliant worker, and if struggling leads to a reward in the hereafter he will not even press for a better standard of living. If emotions are not to be displayed he will not fight back, he will be obedient, he will do as he is told, he will accept what he is offered. It seems not too far afield to suggest that if the Protestant ethic, as we know it, had not existed before, it would have had to be invented with the onset of the industrial revolution.

At this point many readers are objecting, "*My* parents aren't like that!" Admittedly, very few are just "like that," but the description of the ethic is a generalization: it applies a little to almost everyone, and closely to almost none. If it seems not to apply to one's own parents, four possible explanations come to mind. First, it *does* apply to them, but with such subtle manifestations that their child has not yet recognized it; second, it does *not* apply to them but it does to most of the people with whom they share their world; third, it does apply to them, but they are no longer struggling. A view of man which places such importance on the unattainable is one that creates its own victims. Since man is thought to be unavoidably imperfect anyway, countless people subject to this ethic give up the effort to be "good," more or less wryly admit their human frailties, and then relax and try—sometimes with apparent success—to "enjoy" them. Fourth, and most likely, the parents in question—in common with almost everyone else—show some mixture of all three patterns.

The Protestant ethic is so pervasive that it applies

even to people who are neither Protestant nor Christian. A family transplanted to this country from abroad, from another ethic, wastes little time—at most, a generation—in discovering this ethic and trying to adopt it. It is, after all, the ethic of the American success story. And frequently it is just such a family that exerts the greatest pressure on its children to renounce the old beliefs and espouse the new, to become more "American," more accepted, more successful than the old folks have felt. Even when some of the old beliefs are maintained—religious practices, for example—other aspects of the new are avidly sought. Third-generation Italian-Americans show much less of the emotional volatility of the Mediterranean peoples than do first-generation families and eat pasta less frequently than their Anglo-Saxon neighbors; the children of second-generation Jewish families often display puritanical guilts that would have brought forth snorts of derision from their grandparents. But in any event, it is undeniable that the ethic fits American society in general, and that society constitutes the incubator-laboratory.

What effects do this pervasive view of the essential nature of man exert upon the growth of the young human? To answer the question, I shall retrace the biological growth sequence, attempting this time to put it in its cultural setting, and again it must be remembered that I am dealing in generalities that fit no one exactly, but everyone a little. First, the physical stage of growth, from a little after birth to about two and a half: if it is bad form for the human being to admit his animal underpinnings, what happens to the baby who is discovering his body? Most commonly, each step he makes is rewarded with parental smiles of approval, up to a point. His discovery of his hands is a triumph, and so is his discovery of his feet. When he learns to touch his nose with a finger on demand, or to clap his hands, his parents are joyous. But when he finds his genitals gloom descends. The highly intelligent and very well-educated father of a six-month-old boy accosted the family doctor at eight o'clock one morning, with circles under his eyes and a haggard, anxious expression on his face. "Doc," he blurted, "what'll we do? We caught Johnny playing with himself last night and we're afraid he'll turn out to be a homo!" The example seems extreme, but it is probably a fairly common parental response to the genital discovery. And if the objection is consistent, it is easy enough to imagine that the baby's experimentation with this part of his body will be curtailed. In other words, so far as the baby's learning about his genitals is concerned, the average American home is a pretty poor laboratory. This sort of parental response—which, incidentally, can be communicated as clearly with a stunned silence as with a slap of the hand—might provide material for low comedy were it not for its very serious implications and consequences. A baby less than a year old is not very bright, despite the claims of doting grandparents, and he has no way of knowing specifically what the parental response is an objection *to*. Is it an objection to his genitals? Why, then, all the attention to that part of the body every time the diaper is changed? To the baby, this may be the beginning of a major misconception. Because of the continuing and inescapable parental concern with genital cleanliness, the child may gradually gain the impression that the objection is aimed at his *curiosity*, at his need to learn and to experiment. But even if this fate is somehow avoided, it seems almost inescapable that the person subjected to such teaching throughout infancy and childhood will find himself or herself badly hampered with a guilt-laden conception of the genitals when sexual maturation finally occurs.

Genital curiosity is not the only "imperfection" found during the physical stage of growth. Thumb-sucking occurs too, and sometimes receives curative measures as harsh as those directed against touching the genitals. Since it so obviously has to do with physical comfort, thumb-sucking is probably generally considered a sign of "weakness." It should instead be admired for what it really represents—one of the very earliest indications that the baby has within him the spark of independence, that he can provide himself, by himself, with some small measure of the physical solace that earlier he obtained only from the nipple.

Before leaving the physical stage of growth, one brief digression seems indicated. The handling or touching of the genital area by a child in these first years of life is often referred to as infantile masturbation, a term that is grossly misleading. Masturbation involves self-administered gratification of the physical aspects of sexual desire, and sexual desire cannot occur until puberty arrives, with the concomitant maturation of the sexual glandular system. Touching of the genitals *before* puberty is without doubt pleasurable—the area is very richly supplied with nerve-endings whose reason for existence is to provide a pleasurable sensation when stimulated—but until sexual maturation occurs this is not, strictly speaking, a *sexual* pleasure. Babies born into certain other societies, incidentally, where the view of man's nature is different from ours, are commonly and even routinely lulled and comforted by the mother's pats and caresses to the genital area.

This very early encounter between biology and culture illustrates in a nutshell the essence of the Protestant ethic. Here is the baby, thought to be inherently "imperfect"; he possesses a genital that is considered "bad"; he is supposed to have no curiosity concerning it, and the more successfully he suppresses or at least conceals his curiosity, the more nearly "good" he is. But no matter how earnestly he tries, he can never entirely rid himself of that curiosity, any more than he can rid himself of the offending organ. (As a matter of fact, curiosity that is not allowed its satisfaction never dies—it merely goes underground. This appears to account, at least in part, for the fact that American men buy tons of paperback mysteries provided the cover shows a comely young female whose genital area and breasts are almost, but not quite, revealed.) The goal of perfection is unattainable, the animal stigma is ineradicable. Between them can exist, at best, only endless compromise. So the person who wants to accomplish something tangible, once and for all, and be done with it, turns away from the apparent futility of the internal world and directs his attention and his efforts to the simpler realities of the external world. Hence the financial genius who is impotent, the frigid screen star. We shall see further examples of the process as we move through the later stages of growth.

From two and a half to about five the child is in the emotional stage of growth of his sense of self-awareness. As I pointed out in the preceding chapter, he is here concerned with learning to identify his feelings and to express them. And here, too, the ethic comes to bear, even more extensively than it did during the physical stage. The work of Freud has had time by now to render the cultural impact on the physical stage of growth much less severe than it was only a generation ago, but its effect on the emotional stage is at least as vigorous as ever. As the child learns about his feelings of affection, of love, he encounters little if any difficulty at first. Parents are usually free to respond to his demonstrations of affection with their own show of endearment toward him, to encourage him to kiss the parental cheek, to repeat endlessly the "Mummy loves Becky—does Becky love Mummy?" theme. Toward the end of the emotional stage some difficulties frequently make their appearance, but usually they are mild and of relatively little consequence. Most seem to stem from the fact that as the child grows a little older he is interested in studying other people's expressions of affection for one another, and in this regard his parents may be rather inhibited. In other words, they may be better at kissing him than they are at kissing each other.

Certain other of his feelings, however, do not fare so well. Inevitably the child learns to identify his feelings of anger, and just as inevitably they are often directed toward one or both parents and toward siblings. To the child of, say, three, the feeling of anger demands a corresponding action. It is not enough for him to be suddenly mad at his mother because she will not let him play in the dangerous street—he has to demonstrate his wrath by hitting or biting her or by throwing something. And she, if she is in her right mind, will try to stop his hostile action. The difficulty lies in her being able to distinguish between the *act* and the *feeling*: how can she punish the child for biting, but convey to him, at the same time, that it is all right for him to *feel* angry? Most mothers—fathers too, for that matter— cannot make the distinction clearly enough for a three- year-old to understand it, because so many adults in our culture cannot make the distinction clearly enough for themselves. And even if the adult is able to distinguish between feeling and action he too often possesses, and teaches, the conviction that feelings are supposed to be controlled. Probably this conviction stems from the old denial of the animal in us: it is better to be rational, which only the "higher" human being can be, than to be emotional. Certainly the denial of the rightful place of the emotions is related, in part, to our notions of strength and weakness. If accomplishment can occur only in relation to the external world, then of course victory goes to the strong, not to the emotional. But whatever its sources, as a people we do honor to the idea that we control our feelings. For example, one of our commonest folk heroes is the controlled, laconic, strong and silent type, the Gary Cooper figure.

It is obvious nonsense that emotions can be *controlled*. They are reactions to environmental circumstance, as automatic and natural as the feeling of hunger in the absence of food. If a baby is given enough warmth, food, love, attention, and dry clothes, he feels happy. If a three-year-old is blocked in his active exploration of the world, he feels angry. If an eighteen-year-old girl is dressing for her first date with the handsome boy she has admired secretly and from a distance for the past six months, she feels anxious. If her forty-five-year-old father is about to approach, for the first time, an important new client, *he* feels anxious. If her mother has just found a lump in her breast, she thinks at once of cancer and feels fear. And so on—given the circumstances, the feeling arises automatically. It cannot be controlled. What one does about the feeling is another matter, and here the idea of control makes sense. In other words, one can play it cool, but one cannot *feel* cool when the heat is on.

Returning to the angry three-year-old boy, it is easy to see that he *really* is a mad child, and that he is *supposed* to become an un-mad little gentleman. Unfortunately anger is like curiosity: it does not die, either; it too goes underground if it cannot be felt openly. So the three-year-old may grow up to be gentleman, but he will drive his car as if it were a weapon, or he will hate Negroes, or if he has been extra-successful at concealing his anger he may have a stomach ulcer, and then his wife will have to be extra-pleasant and agreeable and give him quantities of milk to drink.

The societal response to anger during the emotional stage of growth is paralleled by the response to anxiety. Here again is a feeling that is inevitable, that is felt when circumstances warrant, that cannot be controlled or turned off on demand. Anxiety is the feeling that accompanies the anticipation of anything new or unfamiliar. It seems likely that the first feeling of anxiety, or at least of a rudimentary form of anxiety, occurs when the baby is first old enough to be aware of separation from his mother. This is a new experience to him, so he reacts by feeling anxious. And every subsequent new experience he faces, throughout life, will evoke some degree of anxiety, but of course with experience, with growing assurance that one usually survives the new, the degree of anxiety diminishes. Unfortunately, anxiety is almost always considered by parents to signify unhappiness, and if anything is truly un-American, it is unhappiness in a child. We Americans are supposed to be happy almost literally from the cradle to the grave, and if a child appears to be unhappy his parents are convinced that they have somehow failed. As with anger, so with anxiety: the parental objection seems to be—and frequently actually is—directed against the feeling itself. In consequence the child *really* is, on occasion, anxious; but he learns that he is *supposed* to be "happy" at all times.

In terms of the laboratory, and of the quality of experimentation that occurs therein, it should be clear that the home governed by the Protestant ethic leaves much to be desired by the child in the emotional stage of growth. How can he experiment with, and learn about, feelings that are supposed not to exist, feelings that must not be expressed even if they do exist? As I have suggested earlier, this stage of growth is particularly important, partly because feelings are relatively intangible and difficult to describe in words, but partly also because during this period a new feeling comes into being, a synthetic feeling in the sense that it is acquired, not inherited. This is the feeling of *guilt*, a peculiar blend of anxiety, resentment, and self-blame which arises when the child does something, or *is* something, that he knows he is not *supposed* to do or be. As the emotional stage of growth comes to its close, at about five, the feeling of guilt is pretty well established. It will remain with the child until and unless he succeeds in achieving the sense of his own identity later, and it will serve to keep him on the path described by society as the straight and narrow, as his increasing independence and ability take him farther from the confines of his parental home.

Perhaps an example will illustrate the point. A youth of seventeen recalled his pleasure, in early childhood, at sitting each morning on the front stoop of his house, watching pupils on their way to the near-by high school. He was particularly pleased by the legs of passing girls, and although some of my psychiatric colleagues, and perhaps some parents, too, would say that such an esthetic interest on the part of a four-year-old would indicate some sort of sexual pathology, I prefer to believe that it could more properly and accurately be accounted for as an example of the frequently unexpected and inexplicable tastes of the very young. In any event, at seventeen he remembered clearly the day, soon after his fifth birthday, on which his esthetic appreciation of those legs was replaced by a guilty feeling, together with a feeling of resentment toward barelegged girls. Suddenly he was not supposed to have such an interest, suddenly *they* were at fault for not wearing stockings. If one is guilty because of a difference between what he is supposed to be and what he really is, it is comforting to blame someone else for making him what he really is. This reaction in a five-year-old is remarkably close to the resentment frequently expressed by chronologically adult men toward exceptionally attractive women—such women are often scornfully called "sexy" because they arouse in men feelings they are not supposed to feel. It is in this fashion that guilt keeps one from straying from the "proper" path.

At about five the child enters the social stage of growth, and here too his experimentation is limited to a degree by cultural dictates. Now he is capable of discovering and learning how to use his capacity for compassion, for *cooperation* with his fellows; but the adults in his world are more likely to be interested in his learning how to *compete*. Perhaps the nine-year-old boy would enjoy helping his pal collect useful junk from the trashcans of the neighborhood, but he may have to do it only after they have both attended Little League practice. Perhaps his eleven-year-old sister wants to spend all her spare time with her best friend, in seclusion from the rest of society; but she will receive more approbation if she seems to be socially popular. A current television commercial for a bread that contains virtually every known vitamin and builds bodies in a surprising number of ways illustrates this point; its announcer reminds parents, "You want your child to be a winner." More often than not, the child left to his own devices cares little, if at all, if he is a winner. He wants to be a part of the childhood group, *within* it, not on top of it. Interestingly, racial prejudices do not exist in children entering the social stage of growth, but they are clearly apparent in children approaching its end; they illuminate as well as anything can the societal subversion of this particular stage. It is little wonder that children in these years answer the question, "Where are you going?" with the monosyllabic "Out," and "What are you going to do?" with "Nothing." This is most likely an ancient and useful defense against the well-meant, if misguided, efforts of parents to civilize the young.

With the arrival of puberty and sexual maturation, the cultural limitation on experimentation reaches its most explicit expression. But now we cannot disparage a puritanical society for being puritanical, because although a thirteen-year-old girl is physically capable of bearing a child, and a fifteen-year-old boy of siring it, neither is capable of the responsibility of parenthood, and a world already filled to overflowing with troubles and people does not need still more unwanted and un-cared-for children. Sexual experimentation, then, must be limited to a *very* considerable degree. But it is fruit-less for a society to decree that youngsters who have reached puberty should be devoid of sexual preoccupa-tions, and a society that does so will only add to the burden of guilt its younger members already carry.

Finally at fifteen or sixteen the cognitive stage begins, and again experimentation specific to the growth that is taking place tends to be officially discouraged. The youth in this stage is introspective, but he is supposed to think of *others*, not of himself. He is moody, he is frequently depressed, he is almost always anxious—and he is supposed to be happy. He thinks of all sorts of important subjects that have nothing to do with his job or his school, he is trying to be objectively critical of his parents when he is supposed to be respectful and obedient. One mother, whom I felt to be rather deserv-ing of criticism, reacted in an extreme manner to the critical attempts of her twenty-year-old son by denounc-ing his university: "Schools should teach a required course in Parent Worship." He is, in short, damned if he does, and equally damned if he doesn't. Whatever useful experimentation he manages to accomplish he does at high cost, and he knows now, if he hadn't noticed before, that it is difficult indeed to grow up.

In summary, the young human being passes through a logical and purposeful biological growth sequence, but the society within which that growth takes place puts in his way obstacles that grow out of and reflect only the societal view of man and his world. The socie-tal aim, of course, is to pass on to the young what the old have painfully learned. The fallacy is that each generation has to do its own learning, in its own time.

The child cannot be protected from the effort of his growth, and the result of attempting to protect him is, in effect, to pass on to him the errors and the misconceptions of his father and his father's father. Society, holding to the Protestant ethic, provides a laboratory for its young experimenters, a laboratory with certain rules and regulations arising from, and dependent upon, that ethic. The more closely they are adhered to, the less the ethic changes with changing times, the more the ethic becomes self-perpetuating. It is commonly said that the family "holds up" society: in this sense, it would perhaps be more accurate to say that the family "holds *back*" society. The cost of such perpetuation is best measured in terms of forsaken opportunity, of inhibited freedom, of unachieved growth. But when a young person enters the cognitive stage, he has it in his own hands to grow as he will, to undo what has inadvertently been done *to* him in the past in the mistaken impression that it was being done *for* him. The next chapter will deal specifically with the cognitive stage, with the opportunities it holds for growth, and with ways in which youth can best utilize it.

REFERENCES

1. O. H. Mowrer, "Psychiatry and Religion," *The Atlantic*, 208:1, July, 1961, p. 91. Critiques of the Protestant ethic are numerous, to say the least. Professor Mowrer's is brief, trenchant, and highly applicable to the purposes

of this book, as his title suggests. See also Erich Fromm, *Escape from Freedom,* New York, Farrar and Rinehart, 1941; and for a fascinating study of Luther, his "emergence," his beliefs, and his work, see E. Erikson, *Young Man Luther,* New York, W. W. Norton, 1958.

4

The Opportunity and
the Challenge of Youth

As poets have always known, the cognitive stage of development is synonymous with youth. If the cognitive capacity is utilized, then youth is fulfilled and gives way imperceptibly but surely to adulthood. But if it is not utilized youth is wasted, its opportunities wither on the vine, and the fruits of adulthood are not tasted. Of course *physical* adulthood occurs, whether one works or plays through the years of youth; but physical adulthood alone is like a frame without a picture. All form and no content, it may look good from a distance, but a closer view discloses its emptiness. If the empty canvas is examined with X-rays it turns out to be not so empty as it appears to the naked eye, but its concealed contents, surprisingly, are the contents of childhood. A seemingly adult housewife, for example, buys a new refrigerator but cannot bring herself to use it until the neighbor women have seen and admired it and have told her, in effect, that it is all right. The dependence of such a person upon the opinions of others is obviously more like a characteristic of childhood than of true adulthood. Or a chronologically adult man spends much of his free time in the company of his fellows at his club, rather than at home with his wife and children. Here the observer may be reminded of the sexually-segregated groupings of children during the social stage of development and wonder if the club member has ever really outgrown his prepubertal years. Masses of people, adult in years only, are *dependent*, in a childish way, on the paternalistic corporation, or the church, or the one-big-family suburban neighborhood. Throngs play games, beyond the need for recreation, and still more escape the anxieties of life through alcohol, television, and the mobility of the family car, running from momentary interest to fleeting thrill with the speed, if not the agility, of a readily distracted and restless six-year-old. In each such example it is easy enough to see the remnants of childhood, remnants that wield a disproportionate measure of control over the life of the person adult in years only.

But while such a fate is common in this society, it is by no means inevitable; and youth is the period of time during which it can be avoided, and at least the outlines of true adulthood can be sketched on the canvas. True, the sketch will be drawn upon a background of childhood and adolescent experience, but in the finished painting visible to the naked eye the background will be only a part of the whole, rather than a concealed and controlling source of misunderstood power. And as a consequence, the lingering dependency of childhood will be replaced, in time, by the responsible *inter*dependence of mature adulthood.

Certain specific actions can be taken in order to utilize most fully the self-cognitive aspect of youth, but before discussing them in detail I should like to re-emphasize two points made in an earlier chapter. First, at intervals during these years the young person finds himself returning—or at least trying to return—to the safety and familiarity of the incubator. As I have pointed out already, such returns are in the nature of the strategic retreat. They provide a brief period of rest and recuperation so that the next advance can be made with renewed vigor. They serve to promote growth, not to retard it: they are a normal feature of the years of youth and are to be used, not feared or ridiculed.

Second, during these years the youth becomes familiar with anxiety. In fact, anxiety could probably be called the most common emotional concomitant of youth, certainly of the early years of youth. In my description of anxiety in Chapter 1 [1] I called it a sense of tension tinged with fear, characterized by certain physical changes, and capable of an extreme range of intensity as well as a great variety of manifestations, many of them camouflaged rather than "pure." I pointed out, as well, that it is the normal emotional response to anything new or unexplored. As one learns to accept the normality of anxiety during the cognitive stage (when there is, without question, more than enough to be anxious about) it tends to appear more consistently in the undisguised form, and later still it tends to lose the element of fear with which it is usually at first associated.

During the years of youth the new experiences that first and most frequently evoke the feeling of anxiety fall under the heading of self-discovery. Once the cognitive capacity has come into being, the young person is prone to relatively sudden and unexpected discoveries of hitherto unseen aspects of himself, and each such discovery is accompanied by its own particular charge of anxiety. Sometimes the anxiety is felt first, with the self-discovery coming to light later on. Perhaps less often it is the self-discovery that comes first, followed quickly by the anxiety; and occasionally both seem to arise at once. But in any event the two are intimately related, and always the anxiety is caused by the self-discovery. Perhaps a few examples will illustrate the point.

> A nineteen-year-old girl in her sophomore year in college said, "This semester has been bad for me— I wish I could write it off as a loss. I saw *Three Faces of Eve* before Christmas and it upset me terribly. The movies shouldn't have moved me that much. I cried and shook, and it's happened a couple of times since, with the same date. I don't know if it's the difference between home and school, or between my date and me." [2]

In this example the anxiety occurred first, precipitated by a movie: "I cried and shook, and it's happened a couple of times since." But already the girl is scouting around in an effort to find the cause of her discomfort, and she seems to be reaching the area I have called self-discovery: "I don't know if it's the difference between home and school, or between my date and me."

> A seventeen-year-old boy during his junior year of high school reported, "Whenever I'm nervous my face breaks out. I sort of know what's causing it— it's trying to be an individual, and that means running against my parents' ideas . . . I can probably tell you right down to the ticket what's wrong, but I don't know what to do about it."

Here anxiety and self-discovery appear to occur together. The boy recognizes his anxiety (a common mixture of the "pure" form and a physically disguised form)—"Whenever I'm *nervous* my face breaks out"— and relates it to his discovery that he is trying to be an individual. We shall discover what he can do about it a little later.

> A nineteen-year-old girl, calm, cool, and collected, reported, "I had a dream about a year ago and I've

never been quite able to forget it. I was standing on a long stairway kissing somebody. I was very close to the person and I realized it was not a man, and when I woke up I realized she looked like a movie actress. For a year I've been trying to figure out what it means . . . Since that dream I've had a repulsion for anything that's sexually abnormal. I'm afraid it's something latent in me."

In this illustration some sort of self-discovery has certainly occurred—"I'm afraid it's something latent in me"—but anxiety has not yet appeared in any clear-cut form. At most we can only infer a mild degree of anxiety; the girl has a "repulsion" and she speaks of being "afraid," but she *acts* neither repulsed nor fearful.

Occasionally the elusive self-discovery that has been causing anxiety makes a dramatic appearance while the victim of the anxiety is describing his discomfort.

A twenty-two-year-old secretary, engaged to be married in six months, came to a psychiatrist's office complaining of nervousness and shaking hands, a difficulty for which she could discover no obvious cause. A few questions revealed the fact that her symptoms of anxiety had coincided with her acceptance of a diamond ring from her fiancé. This news surprised her—the timing of her symptoms had previously escaped her notice—and she responded by suddenly remembering that another symptom had bothered her since she had accepted the ring: whenever she was with the young man her appetite failed her, and on a few such occasions she had even been mildly nauseated. Another question-and-answer sequence followed: "Do you anticipate the sexual aspects of marriage?" "Oh my goodness, yes" —at the same time shaking her head in violent negation. When she was told of her interesting head-shaking response to the question, her jaw dropped, she blushed deeply, and then she laughed and said, "Oh! I didn't!" She devoted the remainder of her first interview to a rapid review of her dating history, describing an unusual degree of prudery, of which she had been aware for some time, and arranged to begin a series of psychiatric interviews.

In this example I have said that the anxiety preceded the self-discovery, but the girl knew of her prudery already. At first glance this seems contradictory. However, it is clear that until this interview she did not relate the prudery to her nervousness, and probably we can say that the effective self-discovery was not the discovery of her prudery, but rather the discovery of its relationship to the anxiety.

Perhaps now the relationship between self-discovery and anxiety is clearer. During the earlier years of youth the presence of anxiety, regardless of its intensity or disguise, is a signal indicating that some aspect of self-discovery lies just over, or right on, the horizon. In other words, anxiety can be utilized as a reminder that the time has come for self-examination. I must stress the point that the anxiety is *normal*. In and of itself it is not a sign of sickness, a symptom that should be "cured" by tranquilizers, alcohol, diversion, or a nice long rest. It is simply the normal indication of growth to come, the growing pain that heralds some change in the direction of maturity. The anxiety associated with self-discovery is cured *only* by getting hold of the self-discovery, making it a matter of conscious knowledge, and placing it in the perspective of one's life to date. The bulk of this chapter will be devoted to the specific actions that can be taken to utilize most fully the self-cognitive aspect of youth, to unearth most readily the self-discoveries that occasion anxiety. It is these specific actions that make it possible for one to "do something about it."

The first step may be called the academic or book-learning step. It involves learning something about the society into which one has been born and in which one has been raised; some guide lines for such an investigation are suggested in Chapter 1. It is easy but wholly inaccurate to assume that the entire world is like the little corner of it one has known, and such an assumption, especially if it is coupled with the notion that society is not subject to objective examination, will not lead to growth. This first step involves, too, learning something about the normal course of growth of the child, the process that was discussed in Chapter 2. These two areas having been covered, it is necessary to put them together, to contrast the beliefs of society with the needs of the child, an effort which was attempted in Chapter 3. All this is book-learning: it can be read, it may or may not be interesting, but it provides a necessary framework for the steps to follow. But by itself it can lead no one toward maturity because it is too abstract and general; it does not involve the reader personally.

The second specific step is a repetition of the first, but this time with a strenuous effort to read one's own experience onto the printed page. This time, if the reader thinks of his parents specifically rather than of society in general, and if he retraces his way through the five steps of growth remembering or trying to guess how *he* fared in *his* family as he passed through each phase, he will probably be surprised, and perhaps a little dismayed, to discover that his memory for his own past is not very long, and he may find too that he is not a particularly good guesser. But the more effort he brings to bear, the more he will find himself becoming involved. Now the book-learning aspect of the task begins to give way to something closer to home.

The third specific step has nothing whatever of the academic about it. This step entails introspection and reflection; it is private and wholly personal. It consists of a search through one's *present* behavior and feelings, attitudes and prejudices, for signs of what might be called unfinished business. Discussing the five steps of growth in Chapter 2, I mentioned that if a given step cannot be dealt with satisfactorily it may crop up later, at a more propitious time. This is that more propitious time, and given our society it is inevitable that some of the growth steps for each young person will have been less than satisfactory. Whatever the gaps or lapses or obstacles of his earlier years, they are being reflected now in his behavior, or in his feelings, or in his attitudes.* As he finds them, he will fill in many of the gaps in his memory which were so apparent while he was struggling with the second of these specific steps.

This matter of unfinished business is of the greatest importance and requires careful elucidation. The search can be systematized to some degree by referring once again to the five stages of growth and by combing the psyche for evidence of unfinished work in each stage. Beginning with the physical stage, the young person can ask himself such questions as, What are my attitudes toward my own body? Do I like it, or am I

---

* The unfinished business to which I refer bears a distinct relationship to Freud's concept of "the return of the repressed." That which has been repressed does indeed return, but during the years of youth it frequently returns in a relatively unclouded state, so that it can be fairly readily identified. When the returning material is disguised, as it so often is in the adult years, it contributes to the symptom-formation of neurosis. It seems likely to me, therefore, that identification of unfinished business during one's youth may well constitute preventive psychiatry, in that I suspect it diminishes the chances of neurotic symptom-formation later.

ashamed of it? What is my level of modesty—is it
greater than, less than, or about the same as that of
most of my contemporaries? Do I think I am too fat or
too thin, too short or too tall, too hairy or not hairy
enough? What conceptions or misconceptions do I have
concerning the function of my body? For example, do
I believe that it is mandatory for everyone to have a
daily bowel movement, and that if this does not occur
the body fills up with poison? Do I believe that menstruation is unclean? When I am tense do I soothe
myself with compulsive eating or sleep to excess? Is my
sexual behavior tinged with simple genital curiosity?
Such questions as these frequently point to the presence
within the currently functioning psyche of leftover bits
of misinformation or misinterpretation acquired during
the physical stage of growth. Simply identifying such
leftovers constitutes a big first step in the process of
getting rid of them, and further steps in the same
process will be considered later.

Similar questions can be asked of oneself with
reference to the emotional stage of growth. Do I feel
inhibited in the expression of my feelings? Am I convinced that I never feel anger? Do I feel embarrassed
about kissing my parents when I return home after an
absence? Do I believe my changes of mood to be extreme? Do I think I am depressed too much of the
time, or angry too much of the time, or anxious too
much of the time? And with reference to the social
stage of growth: Am I socially inhibited, or introverted,
or extroverted? Do I consider my shyness on entering
a room full of strangers abnormal? Do I feel unable to
make friends? Do I get on better with males or females,
people older than I, or younger than I, or my contemporaries? Am I afraid that I am a lone wolf or a
party pooper or a glad-handing phony, or that others
think I am one of these? Going on to the sexual stage
of growth: Do I fear that I am oversexed or under-

sexed? Am I guilty about sexual dreams or nocturnal emissions? Do I believe that masturbation leads to pimples, insanity, or impotence? Am I half convinced that I will turn out to be frigid? In my view, is premarital intercourse a fate worse than death, or its absence the hallmark of the incurable square? Am I secretly afraid of the possibility of homosexuality? Do I have any idea at all of my own sexual anatomy and functioning? Finally, with reference to the cognitive stage of growth: Do I consider myself too introspective, too sensitive, too selfish, too adolescent? Do I feel too impatient, too useless, too uncommitted to the adult world? Am I too rejecting of everything "they" do or stand for?

Clearly, an exhaustive list of such questions would require a great many pages. But, in addition to being of unwieldy length, it would be an unnecessary document. With a little effort each young person can supply his own particular series of questions, and at the least they will serve to identify problem areas, areas of unfinished business. Many of the areas of unfinished business can be identified too by directing attention to the content of dreams, both night dreams and daydreams, and of recurrent topics of preoccupation. For example, a shy eighteen-year-old girl who does not date but who spends hours every week worrying about it might profitably consider her passage through the stages of social and sexual growth, and the twenty-year-old young man who cannot enter a bar without getting in arguments and threatening to fight should certainly try to discover what happened while he was in his emotional stage of growth. Signs of unfinished developmental business are really rather easy to find, once one begins to make the effort, since their expression during the years of youth is automatic and inescapable. Obviously the psychic apparatus "knows" that the cognitive stage of growth, immediately prior to the development of adulthood, is the ideal time to tidy up one's past, and it makes the necessary material richly available to anyone willing to look.

Earlier in this book I referred to the sequence, *discovery—experimentation—mastery*. The identification of unfinished business still residing within the confines of the psyche, as well as the aforementioned book-learning concerning society and human development, are part of what constitutes *discovery* during the cognitive stage of growth. But that same cognitive capacity that enables a young person to discover what he has been in the past makes it equally possible, and equally important, for him to know himself as he exists at the present moment. In other words, the cognitive stage, because it involves *knowing*, is unlike any of the preceding four stages of growth. It brings past and present together in the forefront of consciousness: it brings the young person, at the end of the years of growth, a double dose of discovery. He needs to discover his own past—unless he does, he will have a driven future—but this alone is not enough. He must also discover his own present—unless he does this, he will have a drab future. Discovering the new business of the cognitive stage is the fourth specific step in answering the question, What can one *do* about it?

The self-discoveries that comprise the new business of the cognitive stage are related to the transition from adolescence to adulthood. Finishing the unfinished business leads to the transition, and the transition itself is the new business. Now the youth discovers he is capable of increasing independence from parents and society and their convictions and opinions. He finds himself alone sometimes—indeed, true independence can be born only in the state of aloneness. He finds he is gradually becoming capable of enough self-discipline to get the necessary work done, albeit slowly perhaps and with a certain amount of procrastination. He finds himself increasingly capable of reaching his own measured decisions, and begins to make his own judgments based on his new-found knowledge and experience, learning from his own mistakes, enjoying his own triumphs. Unfortunately, but inevitably, he also discovers the opposite of each of these. He is appalled by the degree of his lingering blind dependence upon the views of others; frequently he cannot tolerate loneliness and will do almost anything to avoid it; sometimes he longs for a tough teacher or boss or parent who will *make* him do whatever it is that at the moment he knows he should do; he will be painfully indecisive; he will feel incapable of making judgments or of possessing opinions; he will try to deny his mistakes; he will deprecate his triumphs. However painful and confusing this may be, it is in the nature of any transition that it contain sets of opposites—but also that the balance between them should undergo progressive change. The accelerating car, in transition between a dead stop and full speed, is going faster than it was, but slower than it will be. Similarly, in the transition from adolescence to adulthood the youth is more grown-up than he was, but less mature than he will be. During this period he will be impatient for time to pass, yet he will feel as if he is getting nowhere. The transition takes time—quite a lot of it, in fact—and during much of the time the young person is neither fish nor fowl, neither child nor adult. He simply has to endure the months or years during which he has loosened his grip on the old but has not yet forged the new. If he wants to grow, he has no alternative. As one nineteen-year-old put it, "I want to reach stability by going through the instability, not by leaning on something."

During this time of fluidity, of shifting balances, of walking through quicksand with pliable legs, it is indeed fortunate that one area of dependable solidity exists. This area is the validity of one's own senses. If a young person sees in himself a streak of childlike dependency, it is there, whether or not the world sees it. If he detects in himself a repugnance for racial injustice, the repugnance is there, regardless of the customs of the land. If his heart speeds up and his abdominal muscles tighten and he breaks into a nervous sweat whenever his date exhibits her affection for him, his anxiety is there and its presence cannot be doubted. What one sees or hears is real and reliable. One's *interpretation* of it may be faulty, but the experiencing of it is unimpeachable. It is this fact that makes experimentation possible, and now, at long last, I shall turn my attention from the *discovery* of the cognitive stage to the next step, *experimentation*.

Experimenting with one's new discoveries constitutes the fifth specific action, and without it the discoveries alone, no matter how many or how brilliant, cannot bring anyone to the goal of maturity. Self-discovery evokes anxiety, as I have mentioned, and experimentation evokes more. It is painful to have to admit to oneself that father is less than perfect. It is substantially more painful, or at least more frightening, to try to stand up to him when he is not on his best behavior and tell him what one honestly thinks of him on such occasions. It is evocative of anxiety to discover that one is not as independent as one thinks one should be, and it is evocative of significantly more anxiety to try to survive, on one's own, a weekend or a few days in a strange city in an experimental effort to enhance one's degree of independence. But without experimentation there can be no mastery—"If you don't bet, you can't win"—and with experimentation there will be losses, failures, and pain. Anxiety is the price of growth, and courage its prerequisite. Nowhere is this more clearly evident than in the experimentation of youth.

The discoveries of the cognitive stage fall into the

two categories of the old and the new, and experimentation follows suit. Experimentation with newly discovered unfinished business occurs also automatically. If a young person discovers in himself an inability to express resentment because he was brought up to be "nice," he will find himself becoming increasingly uncomfortable in situations that warrant resentment. For example, he may realize within himself a growing intolerance of anti-Semitic remarks and jokes until finally, at a party, he surprises himself, and his friends, by snapping at the teller of such a story. If he has decided he was brought up to be excessively competitive he will feel increasingly uncomfortable in competitive situations and finally he will find himself saying "the hell with it," letting others compete as they will while he sits under a tree. If it occurs to him that his knowledge of sexual anatomy is strikingly limited he will make an effort to broaden it. The point to be made here is that once the unfinished business has been identified one tends to experiment with it whether one makes a deliberate effort or not.

In the case of experimentation with the *new* business of the cognitive stage, a rather different situation prevails. Now there is less of the automatic; hence more of the deliberate is required. If an eighteen-year-old has a tentative political opinion contrary to those of his parents, he will probably have to make something of an internal effort, a deliberate effort, to "try it out" on the parents. If he believes he is finally independent enough to travel alone to the city three hundred miles away, he will have to make the necessary plans and arrangements, again quite deliberately. If during his junior year in college he discovers that his field of interest is not what he had previously believed it to be, he will have to go to a good deal of bother to change his major; or if he has a job that ceases to hold his interest he will have to make an effort—and run the risk of joblessness—to find one that might be better. Obviously experimentation involves risk, and the more deliberate—that is, the less automatic—the experimentation, the more the risk becomes a matter of the experimenter's own responsibility; at the same time, however, the more the gains of experimentation become the experimenter's own reward.

Throughout all this experimentation it is well to keep two words in mind: *extreme* and *tentative*. All experimentation involves alternation between extremes, and as an experiment continues the distance between extremes narrows. For example, if a biochemist wants to discover the amount of Vitamin C a mouse needs for best health, he will begin by feeding one group of mice what he hopes is too much Vitamin C, and another group too little. Then he will systematically reduce the amount fed to the first group, and increase that fed to the second, until neither group shows evidence of overdose or insufficiency. He will then have a *tentative* answer to his question. But perhaps his strain of mice has different Vitamin C requirements from other strains, perhaps he was unaware that his supply of Vitamin C contained impurities that affected his findings, perhaps his mouse food contained Vitamin C without his knowing it. Drawing a parallel with the youthful experimenter, we can describe his beginning struggle with the question of independence as alternating between the extremes of wild and reckless independence and three-year-old tearful dependence. Gradually the extremes will come closer together, and finally he will be able to say, tentatively, "I am independent enough." But his answer is *tentative* because he has not been able to test his degree of independence in many different situations, and he cannot know how it will stand up in contexts not yet experienced. Similarly, in experimenting with his ability to get on with girls, the sixteen- or seventeen-year-old boy is likely to alternate between being "snowed" and being utterly indifferent. Later the extremes may be those of loving well but not wisely, on the one hand, and wisely but not very well, on the other. And finally the tentative answer will emerge: "I *think* I can get along well enough with girls." It can still be only a tentative answer, however, because he has not yet tried living in the intimacy and responsibility of marriage.

In short, experimentation cannot occur without alternation between extremes, and the commitments arrived at during the years of youth are of necessity tentative commitments. Both of these statements run counter to many convictions of contemporary American society, but they are nonetheless true. If one is a good experimenter he will experience unfashionable extremes of behavior and of feeling, and he will be considered remiss in not possessing firm, rigid, and unshakable commitments to a variety of social roles and societal beliefs. In time the extremes will become much less extreme, and in time many of the tentative commitments will have given way to enduring principles. And while the young person may be criticized for having achieved those principles slowly, they will be *his*, and they will have been based upon his own hard-won experience, upon his own course of experimentation. They may coincide in the long run with familial and societal beliefs—indeed, many will—but they will be a great deal more than hand-me-down beliefs.

Finally, one word of caution with regard to experimentation: it *must* be based upon its prerequisite, discovery. Discovery without experimentation may lead to encyclopedic knowledge, but it cannot bring one to maturity; and experimentation without discovery, premature or hasty or impulsive experimentation, leads only to unnecessary injury. The example of the baby who plays with matches is as apt as it is hoary.

One more specific action of the cognitive stage remains to be mentioned, and it may be called supportive in nature. One can talk about one's discoveries and about one's experimentation, both with contemporaries attempting the same sort of growth and with knowledgeable and objective adults who have passed the same way earlier. In this regard the bull session is of inestimable value. It not only affords the opportunity to discover that one has company in these struggles, but it provides, as well, a forum within which one can experiment with many new-found and newly emergent ideas—especially those having to do with such vital issues as religion, politics, ethics, the family, education, sex and marriage. And by bull session I mean a forum for *honest* discourse that is free of the smug statements, unquestioned and unquestioning, of the conformer, and free as well of the daring or insulting bragging of the rebel.

In summation, the work of the cognitive stage can be outlined as follows:

A. Discovery
    1. Survey of society, of the course of human growth, and of the interaction between the two.
    2. The relationship of one's own history to this survey.
    3. The search for one's own unfinished business.
B. Experimentation.
C. Support.

What is taken from the years of youth will be in proportion to what is put into them. It is my conviction that any young person who is willing to flesh out this outline for himself, with sufficient dedication to the project, cannot avoid the achievement of true, mature adulthood. However, it is not a job to be done in the time it takes to read a book, or in a week or a month or a year. If the job is begun at eighteen, it *can* be essentially finished by the early twenties, but more likely it will drag on more slowly than that. Even for the highly dedicated youth the years of transition are not easy, and there are not many forces within our society designed to give support to the young people who are striving for this measure of maturity. Quite the contrary, in fact: people who honestly make this effort are all too commonly accused of selfishness, of irresponsibility, of postponement of adult obligations.* They are called, at best, "slow bloomers" (probably there are,

* I have made no effort to distinguish in these pages between young men and young women because the *nature* of the search for identity is the same for each. The *timing* of the search, however, and the relative ease with which it is conducted are not the same. This difference is cultural rather than biological in origin, and it seems likely that it will diminish gradually as time passes. For the boy, the search for identity seems to start later, to progress more slowly, and to be, in general, more painful than it is for the girl. One factor contributing to this situation is the pressure of society, which demands of the boy or young man some sort of vocational commitment, the acquisition of a collection of skills that will enable him to earn a living, during the years of youth. Certainly there is no better time for him to learn such things; already the intricacy of our technological society painfully prolongs the time he must spend learning how to make a living, and the process can hardly be put off until later. But it is my impression that much too much emphasis is placed upon such learning, that the young man is subjected to too much competitive pressure to succeed in this area, so that he is left with neither time nor energy to seek his own identity during these years. Another factor that doubtless inhibits the psychological growth of the young male is the cultural stereotype that such activities as introspection and reflection, and such attributes as sensitivity, are "unmasculine." Girls too are often criticized for possessing these characteristics, but for them it is a relatively tolerant criticism: they shouldn't do such things, but then they are girls, and girls are like that. And sometimes, it should be added, they are actually encouraged in such pursuits because girls are considered the "culture carriers." For boys, however, the criticism is more potent: it has teeth in it. Not only shouldn't boys do such things, but if they do, they must often face the judgment that they are not entirely masculine—even though the majority of renowned thinkers, philosophers, poets, artists, and musicians are men. With luck, a boy may achieve his psychological maturity later, and the job *can* be done later; but with more difficulty and, probably, more slowly than if it had been included among the efforts of his youth.

in fact, only slow bloomers and nonbloomers) and at worst "no-goods." They are charged with lack of decisiveness, they hear until they are sick of it "I told you so" and "Why can't you be like so-and-so?" And at the same time they must learn to bear their own growing pains, their depressions and doubts and fears and anxieties, in lonely silence, except for those rare moments when some of them can be shared with a kindred spirit.

But the rewards of mature adulthood are worth it all. The mature adult knows a sacred cow when he sees one. He can distinguish between a Principle with a capital P and an absurd myth more accepted than questioned. He knows the difference between what he *wants* to do and what he is merely supposed to do. He knows that first things come first, and he knows what his own first things are. He knows himself, he knows his world, and more—he knows an ethical, responsible, and joyous way for him to live in it.

In an earlier day well-meaning and enlightened parents, who knew their children were sufficiently grown to go forth on their own responsibility, often said, "Let your conscience be your guide." The idea, of course, was that the conscience would let its possessor know if his anticipated action would be right or wrong in the appraisal of his elders. Unhappily, that parental benediction no longer works—the world is changing so rapidly that what was right for us elders may be wrong for youth; but nobody can know until youth gets there. And the only way for youth to appraise it will be in terms of ability to distinguish reality as it exists, from a basis of maturity. So the benediction must be rephrased: "Let your *anxiety* be your guide." When anxiety arises, the young person will know that he has not yet learned something that needs to be learned, or having learned it, he has not yet made sufficient effort to try it out on the world in order to test its validity.

Discover, experiment, and grow. This is the opportunity of youth—and its responsibility.[3] The young person who shirks this responsibility is like the voter too lazy to vote: he has no right to complain if the election turns out wrong. But it is a weighty responsibility, one that can neither be assigned nor assumed casually. And no matter how carefully or completely the assignment is specified, assignment alone is not enough. It must be accompanied by discussion and explanation of those particular aspects of life that are most widely misunderstood, misconstrued, or misinterpreted in contemporary American society: sex, anger, and anxiety. It is to this end that the three following chapters are directed.

REFERENCES

1. See Chapter 1, p. 5.
2. The clinical examples used in this chapter appeared earlier, in somewhat different form, in *Psychiatry, Journal for the Study of Interpersonal Processes* (R. E. Nixon, "An Approach to the Dynamics of Growth in Adolescence," *Psychiatry*, 24:1, Feb. 1961). I wish to thank the editors of that journal for their permission to use this material here.
3. A reading of Mowrer's article, cited in Reference no. 1, Chapter 3, will point out the incompatibility of this notion of personal *responsibility* with conventional views of the Protestant ethic. At the risk of appearing repe-

titious, but in the hope of forestalling charges of sacrilege, I stress again my conviction that this ethic, as it seems currently to be understood, represents a distortion of the teachings of Christ and of the underlying validity of Christianity. See Chapter 3, pp. 49-50.

5

Sex or Guilt

It is a temptation to end this book here, having presented my ideas about how young people can pursue the growth struggles of youth. The effort would be incomplete, however, without sketching in, in greater detail, what it is that has to be struggled *against*. Since growth comes naturally, it follows that the struggle must be against something unnatural, something not inherent in the human species. I shall attempt to point out that the something unnatural has to do with certain cultural misconceptions concerning the nature of man and how to bring him from birth to maturity. As this discussion unfolds, it must be kept in mind that the young human being is a particularly difficult creature to rear—in so many ways his physical capacities, during the years of growth, outstrip his capacities for judgment—and in any culture the first concern must be some technique of child-rearing that will keep the child alive until he grows up. The two-year-old, fully capable of playing on his own, must be kept from playing in the middle of a superhighway, and the husky six-year-old from taking the family axe to his little sister. In other words, I shall not be complaining about the fact that restrictions are placed by society on the activities of the young. My complaints and criticisms will be leveled rather at certain modes of restrictions in contemporary American society, and the cultural beliefs upon which they are founded.

If the theme or leitmotif of growth is discovery—experimentation—mastery, the theme of the cultural restrictions I am about to discuss is *discovery—feeling of guilt—suppression.* The four-year-old, in his exploratory zeal, discovers the excitement of the superhighway. If the speed and noise of the traffic do not dissuade him, there is a good chance that a feeling of guilt will—he has been told many times not to play on, or even near, the highway—and he will suppress his interest in that particular location for play. Obviously this is a splendid arrangement for protecting the child. He cannot be accompanied by responsible adults all the time, but his bones will be spared if, under such circumstance, he acts as if he remembers the parental dictum, feels guilty for having considered playing in the forbidden place, and turns back. Unfortunately, however, the sense of guilt is very readily instilled in the child. It can easily be used to provide control where freedom to experiment would be more appropriate, and it is so used—or, more accurately, misused and even

---

* For a brief description of the sense in which I am using the word *suppression*, see pp. 101-103. I am aware, of course, of the Freudian ideal of successful suppression (more accurately, repression), as for example in the phenomenon of sublimation; but I have never been able to convince myself that such a process actually does or can occur. The notion that any human experience or memory or even memory trace can be so successfully, thoroughly, and permanently repressed that it no longer exists except in the form of a constructive and no longer recognizable transformation impresses me as one that seriously underestimates (or perhaps overestimates) the capabilities of the human brain. In short, I believe Freud was entirely correct and realistic when he spoke of the "return of the repressed" as if it were inevitable, and I suspect he was attempting to construct a happy ending to the theory of compromise when he "invented" sublimation.

abused—in three specific areas of child-rearing in contemporary America. These areas have to do with sex,
anger, and anxiety.

As I indicated earlier, the feeling of guilt is an *acquired* feeling.[1] The baby is not born with it; he must
learn it, and learn it he does. Usually it is well established and functioning smoothly by the sixth year.
Essentially, the feeling of guilt is a feeling of particular
blameworthiness: he who feels guilty blames himself
for having done or contemplated something considered
wrong by those upon whom he is dependent. During
the first five or six years of life guilt gradually becomes
internalized. For example, at first the baby learns not to
throw his cup of milk because, if he does, his mother
will scold him or slap him. Later—say at two and a half
—he refrains from throwing the cup, even though he is
angry and would like to throw it, not because his
mother is standing over him with upraised hand, but
because his mother, who may be out of sight in another
part of the house, would certainly punish him if he
did. Still later, at six or seven, he will not throw the
cup because the voice of his own conscience tells him
he had better not, that it is "wrong." By this age, in
other words, the child knows what is "right" and what
is "wrong." He knows it in his own head, and has long
since lost sight of the fact that the definitions of right
and wrong were originally placed in his head by his
parents.

Referring back to the definition of guilt, it is worth-
while to stress the phrase "those upon whom he is dependent." So long as the child is dependent he has no
choice in the long run but to espouse the beliefs of
those without whose continued care he cannot exist. In
the course of the early years it is perhaps inevitable that
parents convey to the child the notion that they will
love and care for him when he obeys and pleases them,
but that love and care may be withdrawn when he dis-

obeys. Whether this idea is communicated explicitly, by cruel parents, or very subtly, by oversolicitous parents, appears to make little if any difference to the child. He gets the message, he learns the rules about right and wrong, he acquires the capacity to feel guilt. As a technique for controlling the growing child the use of guilt is probably unsurpassed. Once the sense of guilt has been internalized it works efficiently, automatically, and economically, even in the absence of the authorities who established the definitions of right and wrong.* And the convenience to the child of such a mode of control should not be overlooked. It allows him to learn, relatively quickly, those areas in which he will not be able to spend much of his time or energy, it tends to minimize his having to go through a lengthy period of repeating the same error and being punished for it, and it protects his time for investment in other growth activities.

But despite its obvious efficacy, guilt as a controlling mechanism is subject to two grave faults. First, we know how to teach it to the child who is dependent enough upon adult judgment to need it, but we do not know as much about how to help the no longer so dependent youth to unlearn it or to utilize it for growth. The parental or societal concept of right and wrong is generally good enough for the growing child; but it is not usually good enough for the newly-arrived adult who

* The convenience to society of control-by-guilt was described sixty years ago: "In the morality of the individual, society creates for itself an organ which is not only more fundamentally operative than law and custom, but which also spares society the different sorts of costs involved in these institutions. Hence the tendency of society to satisfy its demands as cheaply as possible results in appeals to 'good conscience,' through which the individual pays to himself the wages for his righteousness, which otherwise would probably have to be assured to him through law or custom." (G. Simmel, "The Number of Members as Determining the Sociological Form of the Group," *American Journal of Sociology*, 1902, 8, 1-46, 19 [footnote].)

has it within his own powers to establish a new order
of right and wrong, fitting more precisely the conditions
of the world of his adulthood. Particularly during times
of rapid change, the inability of the new generation to
loosen its grip upon the world view of the old makes
for a rapidly growing cultural lag between world view
and reality, it is at least conceivable that a society in
which this happened could find itself overwhelmed by
an external reality it simply failed to see.* Secondly,
guilt as a controlling mechanism is dependent upon the
ability of the authorities who define right and wrong
to sense reality. If sexual behavior in *every* context is
seen as "wrong," society will spawn young people
crippled, in some fashion and to some degree, in the
sexual behavior without which they cannot perpetuate
society. If the child learns that it is wrong to feel anger,
he will be unable, later on, to combat effectively such
angering forces as social injustice, and such angering
people as venal holders of public office.

Much of the discussion of the preceding chapter
dealt with a way—I suspect *the* way—to outgrow the
need for control-by-guilt, a way characterized by the
courageous discovery of and experimentation with the
products of one's own independent experience. It will
be my effort now to examine the three specific areas
mentioned previously to determine the extent to which
the common cultural view of them fails to accord with
reality. In so doing I shall identify what may be called
unnecessary or unrealistic guilt, guilt frequently gene-
rated during the process of child-rearing that "protects"
the child from something he is better off being ex-
posed to, guilt that too often is carried over, un-

* I do not intend here a plea for the establishment of mere
relativism or of a pattern of amoral opportunism, but rather to
point out that a sensible and flexible pragmatism, in the face
of constant change, is preferable to blind reliance on patterns
applicable to the vanished past.

examined and uncriticized, into the years of chronological adulthood.

Beginning with the question of sex, I shall return for a moment to the first, or physical, stage of growth and recall that it is common practice for parents to be embarrassed by and therefore to inhibit the baby's discovery of his own genitals. A gentle slap on the hand of an anatomist of six months, or the tying of the hands of a two-year-old to the crib sides (yes, it actually happens) may seem a very long way from sexual inhibition in the thirty-year-old or psychosis during the menopause. Yet it is all too commonly the first step in the development of both. Since the organs that make up the reproductive complex do not come into their maturity until puberty, it is clearly unrealistic to read into the baby, or the child of two or of eight, sexual feelings, strivings, or desires. Certainly two normally curious siblings, one male and one female, somewhere between ages two and five, if they are bathed together in the same tub, may get the obvious idea that the penis of the one might fit into the vaginal orifice of the other. At that age, however, such an observation is no more sexual in nature than the very similar observation that Johnny's finger will fit into Judy's nostril. But most American parents would treat the two observations very differently: they read into the first, but not the second, the wealth of sexual associations that they, as adults, would have under similar circumstances. These are obviously *not* the thoughts the two children in the tub possess. Realistically or not, however, sexual associations of the adult are ascribed to the genital curiosity of the child, and the child begins to learn that genital curiosity is "wrong." Of course, the parental or societal aim is not the instillation of a sense of guilt in order to control genital curiosity. It is rather to control later, mature sexual behavior in the thirteen- or fourteen- or fifteen-year-old who is far from ready for the responsibilities of parenthood. Obviously such control is essential, and perhaps guilt is as good a means of control as any other, at least up to a point that will be mentioned later. But to confuse the reality of the fourth, or sexual, stage of development with that of the first, or physical, stage leads inevitably to the creation of a heavy burden of unnecessary, unrealistic and unnatural guilt that very, very commonly complicates the sexual aspects of life for the adult. As Kinsey and many others have shown, in this society psychosexual *immaturity* in the adult is the rule, and maturity the exception. It seems fair enough to say that the control of sexual behavior by affixing guilt to genital curiosity at the beginning of life works, if anything, *too* well.

But the cost in adult psychosexual immaturity is not the only result of unnecessary guilt, nor is it even the worst. As I suggested earlier, the baby is not very good at discovering what the fuss is all about, and if his genital curiosity is inhibited he does not realize that the reason for it all is to protect him from premature paternity. In fact, it is much more likely that he will misinterpret its aim and decide that what is "wrong" is not just his genital or his curiosity concerning it, but perhaps his whole body or maybe even his very curiosity. So we pay the price for this unnecessary guilt not only in widespread marital unhappiness. We pay for it also in widespread self-destructive activity—witness the slaughter on our highways—for the body that evokes guilt is hardly a body to take care of. And, greatest tragedy of all, we also pay the price of stifled curiosity. Discovery of genital area—feeling of guilt—suppression of adult sexuality, of sensible concern for the body, even of curiosity in other areas. The alternative is discovery of genital area—experimentation—mastery.*

* In the sequence discovery—experimentation—mastery I am using *mastery* to signify proficiency in dealing with what has been discovered. In the case of the infant's discovery of his genital

There seems little reason to wonder which is the better process. In short, the societal notion that the genital curiosity of childhood contains associations typical of adult sexuality is far from realistic, and its application to child-rearing practices gives rise to unnecessary, unnatural guilt the consequences of which are far-reaching and exorbitantly expensive, both to the individual sufferer and to society as a whole. But at the same time it *does* seem to be a system that limits premature parenthood.

Premature parenthood is obviously a state of affairs to be avoided, and doubtless during the early years of adolescence, when parenthood is a possibility, some measure of external control is needed. The question is, is our approach to the problem, control by suppression of genital curiosity, the best or the only approach? It is certainly not the only approach, and it seems highly questionable that it is the best. So far as I know, premature parenthood occurs no more frequently in Sweden than it does here, and possibly less frequently, even though in Sweden much less emphasis is placed on the suppression of genital curiosity. However, regardless of facts, any questioning of the status quo, especially in an area as sensitive as this one, brings forth howls of protest and fright. Many people, including some "experts," will contend most desperately that if the baby is allowed his genital curiosity he will end up unprincipled and uncivilized—a sexual menace—

---

region, mastery occurs when he has become familiar with the appearance of the region, with the feelings associated with it, with the bodily functions mediated by it, with the necessary techniques for its cleanliness. Obviously such mastery requires the passage of some time, it cannot occur in the presence of parental objections and restrictions, and it has nothing to do with sex. And with this area of discovery, as with all others, once mastery has been achieved the chapter is closed. The child who is allowed to master the discovery of the genital area will not thereafter find it a source of continuing and never-satisfied curiosity.

at nineteen or twenty, or at sixteen, or maybe even earlier.

It seems logical to me to suppose that if children were allowed their genital curiosity they would relatively soon, certainly by four or five, exhaust its possibilities for exploration and experimentation—and then turn their attention to a world full of more pressing and interesting matters, until the approach of puberty and the sexual stage of development. If they were then taught the facts of life by parents unembarrassed by sex and concerned for the welfare of their children (and I do not mean by the simple expedient of handing out the little pamphlet published by a manufacturer of sanitary napkins) I would anticipate no significant increase in our national rate of premature parenthood. Such concerned and unembarrassed teaching, by parents, should suffice to see the young ones through the earlier reaches of adolescence and on to the point at which they can take over control of their own sexuality. Certainly the young adolescent is still sufficiently dependent upon parental care and love to take seriously the sequence discovery of reproductive ability—feeling of guilt—suppression of reproductive ability.

Instruction of this sort would not only serve to limit premature parenthood, but in addition it would leave the adolescent free to explore and experiment with the many other aspects of sexuality which are not, in reality, dangerous either for the individual or society. Here I have reference to such capacities as tenderness, affection, concern for another, the ability to know another intimately and to share oneself with another. I hold no brief for "free love," and any stirring of the passions by close physical contact had certainly better be withheld until the ability to know, to share, to understand, and even to love has been reasonably established. For one so dedicated as I to the value of experimentation it of course follows that physical experimentation is inevitable and essential; but it should come later, not earlier, and it need not be complicated by a great charge of genital curiosity left over and still unsatisfied from the earliest years of life.

By physical experimentation I mean, of course, experimentation over the entire range of physical modes of expressing affection. This is a very long continuum, beginning with hand-holding and culminating with sexual intercourse between two people who love, and are committed to, each other. But it implies another area of experimentation, too: that which leads to the capacity for love, for commitment, for knowledge of another. This is the work of the cognitive stage of development, discussed in the preceding chapter. Since the cognitive stage occurs later than the sexual stage, it follows that experimentation with the physical aspects of sex needs somehow to be integrated with the developmental work of the cognitive stage. Otherwise intercourse is only a physical experience, devoid of love, of concern, of emotional fulfillment. In the dating patterns of youth very much more time, effort, and anguish are devoted to the work of the cognitive stage than to sexual experimentation. The need to know one another, emotionally and intellectually, takes precedence over the need to establish sexual compatibility; but despite this difference in priority the two aims coexist in time. A nineteen-year-old girl summed up the difficulties of this aspect of growth by saying, "I hope Ted is the last of the series where I have to learn that physical intimacy has to be out of it until you're in it every other way. It's such a cart-before-the-horse sort of thing."

In practice, how do we in contemporary America deal with the question of sexual activity? First we try to control it by equating genital curiosity, in infancy and childhood, with guilt. Then, around the time the child comes to puberty, we mutter vague sounds about birds and bees, facts of life, where do babies come from, and the like, usually with red faces and feeling the need for an extra highball. Following the lead of our own guilt we try to ignore the fact that if our boy or girl wants more or better information, he or she will turn to whatever other kids are available and the line between information and misinformation will be blurred, to say the least. This accomplished, we immediately set about the complicated business of preparing the poor child for a life of social success, of dating proficiency and popularity. Clothes are bought, dancing and driving are learned, drinking is taught, dating is encouraged —maybe only in groups, at first, and with a lot of parental chaperonage, but this doesn't last long—and the degree of freedom is steadily increased.[2] By sixteen or seventeen or eighteen many, and probably most, American teen-agers have all the freedom and privacy they need for sexual experimentation, but their knowledge about sex is primitive and pathetic. *Discovery-experimentation-mastery*: the formula still holds, but if its first component, discovery (or knowledge), is insufficient, then experimentation becomes dangerous and mastery may be replaced by disaster. The ten-year-old boy is a case in point: he has a chemistry set, and he is an avid experimenter. Because his knowledge of chemistry is less than profound his homemade rocket blows the roof off the house. Parents and society have given the American teen-ager the idea that sex in general is somehow wrong (but "everybody does it"); they have taught him almost nothing specific about it; but they provide him with almost unlimited freedom to experiment with it. Then they evince surprise when the roof disappears, or to be more accurate, when the floor falls out from under them.

Nothing a young person can do at this point will change the way he was brought up. If, as is probably the

case, he acquired the usual degree of guilt in relation
to genital curiosity and the usual paucity of sexual
education thereafter and now possesses the usual degree of freedom to experiment with the sexuality he
knows so little about, he can of course get on with the
job. But he has another choice as well, and it may strike
him as preferable. In spite of his embarrassment he can
ask his questions concerning sex; and if he does so he
will have gone far toward overcoming the old unnecessary guilt. He can ask his questions of the family
doctor, if he can catch him when he has time to answer,
or he can ask them of a biology teacher, or of any reasonably enlightened adult. If he encounters the red face
of adult embarrassment he should excuse himself and
try someone else. He can also read books on the subject
—and again he may have to contend with his own embarrassment. It is not easy to ask a librarian for a book
on the locked shelves, but it can be done. Of course it
is a little too easy to find so-called "sex books" that are
sensational, salacious, or downright pornographic, but
there are good ones, too.[3] And obviously the young person can, he will, he must do his own experimenting. For
his own sake, he should do everything he can to keep
his experimentation geared to his knowledge.

I hasten to point out that this recommendation to
experiment is not a wild and reckless position. It is the
point in the evolution of sexual control that we have
presently reached, and if it is a position that seems to
some reckless or dangerous or subversive or depraved,
its history is visible and inevitable. Some pages back I
mentioned that guilt is probably an effective means of
controlling sexual behavior *up to a point*. That point
occurs somewhere in middle or late adolescence, at
a time when physical maturation has combined with
sufficient experience of life in general to make marriage,
and hence parenthood, feasible, if not yet very sensible.
From that point on, until marriage becomes a sensible

possibility, guilt is no longer an effective means of control. In an earlier day it was, thanks to social forces that are no longer present. For a long time the guilt attached to genital curiosity saved the innocence of the young adolescent, and then its reinforcement first by the church and later by secular society continued that protection until such time as the authorities decreed marriage to be possible. The time lag, of course, between puberty and marriageability was not as long two or three hundred years ago, or even fifty years ago, as it is now, and doubtless this fact contributed to the success of the externally-imposed control of sexuality. Certainly that control was generally successful: young people who transgressed, who married prematurely or whose relationship in some other way failed to receive the sanction of church or society, were virtually ostracized. Their punishment was great enough to serve as a potent deterrent, particularly since very little precedent in unsanctioned unions was visible.

In those times, too, emergence from the social incubator was a very different matter. At most, the young person emerged only far enough to live in a different house, but in the same town; and at the least, he emerged only enough to be allowed to bring his bride into his parents' home. It is easy enough to understand the strength of the socially controlling, inhibiting forces under such circumstances—even today, most young people are familiar with the fact that they feel like two different people at home and away, that their behavior sometimes differs markedly in the two settings.

The work of Darwin, a century ago, contributed indirectly and inadvertently to the undermining of the church's authority to enforce the external imposition of sexual control, and that of Freud, a half century later, has contributed similarly to an undermining of the authority of secular society. The result of these sweeping and, in fact, revolutionary changes is that in contemporary America control by guilt (in connection with genital curiosity) is exercised until a certain point in middle-to-late adolescence, and then suddenly no effective mode of externally imposed control exists. It is partly because of our lack of effectively controlling religious or secular institutions that we sometimes call ourselves a society without guiding principles, without goals, even without morals. The fact of the matter is, however, that we have outgrown the old providers of principles, goals, and morals, and we have not yet come to the point where we can discern the new. We might do better to search for clues to the new than to indulge ourselves in the bathos of national self-criticism, of self-righteous tearful regret that the milk is spilled. It is my own impression that the new mode of control of sexual behavior that we are approaching will be vastly better than the old. But since it is new we, as a society, approach it apprehensively, with a sort of societal anxiety, just as the growing child approaches the next new step in his development with his own personal anxiety.

We are afraid that the new mode of control is totally relativistic, entirely shorn of the comfort and security of moral absolutes, but in my view we are wrong. When I was young the absolutes were spelled out, but they were not defined. A sign high on the wall of the university gymnasium read, "Don't smoke, smoking leads to drinking. Don't drink, drinking leads to petting. Don't pet, petting leads to something else." Today the absolutes have not yet been spelled out, but they are in process of being defined. The first one has to do with pregnancy: the youthful generation is aware of the responsibility of pregnancy, and they intend their sexual gropings to stop short of that result until and unless they themselves are ready to assume the responsibility. And the second absolute has to do with man's relationship to his fellow man. The youthful generation does not condone sex for the sake of controlling, manipulating, or exploiting and hurting others, or as a defense against others, or as a means of aggrandizing oneself, or as a dehumanized source of "kicks." In short, the young are trying to discover the appropriate place of sex in the mature life, and in their efforts they have pared down the moral absolutes to concrete issues. No longer can they be told, "Don't pet, petting leads to other things"; no longer can they be handed a ready-drawn and arbitrary line of demarcation beyond which "good" people do not go. In effect, they are rejecting an old and rather fuzzy morality for one that is new, clear, and hard. They are leaving behind a relativistic morality —"Don't do what others don't do"—in favor of one that is absolute: "Don't do what we all know is wrong." [4]

I believe the new mode of sexual control is here already, but it is so new that it is not yet generally visible, and all the bugs have not been worked out of it yet. The fact that it is as yet far from perfect is in-controvertible, but then it is being forged by a new generation of courageous youth who are inventing it as they go. They are making mistakes, some of them pretty drastic, but mistake-making is in the nature of learning by experience. In contrast with the old mode of externally imposed control, the new one is a mode of *internal* control. It works on a basis of what the individual *feels* is right as a result of his own experience, rather than on a basis of what he has been *told* is right —rules drawn from the handed-down experience of someone else, in a different place and at a different time. It is a mode of control that is difficult to achieve, costly, and dangerous: the individual may make mistakes. The old mode, however, was difficult to maintain, extremely costly, and far more dangerous. I shall expand this comment later.

Given almost unlimited freedom, the reasonably

healthy adolescent, no matter how guilty, will sooner or later take advantage of it. It is out of this setting of freedom, of opportunity to experiment, that the new mode of control is arising. The adult world, regardless of its doubts and fears and worries, cannot legitimately object to what youth is doing with its freedom, since it is the adults who made it possible. Youth, in its turn, can only use its freedom constructively. It is for this reason that I have said that young people will, and must, do their own experimenting, but that they owe it to themselves to keep the experimentation geared to their knowledge. The more one knows, the more nearly successful the experiment and the sooner the mastery. If a youth has courage enough to seek out the information he needs, and then the greater courage to find out how it works, he will achieve an internal mode of control of his sexual behavior that will fit him and his particular circumstances and times with far greater precision than could be expected of any externally imposed mode of control, no matter how wise its proponent. And there is a good chance that if he does this during his years of youth he will discover, later, a way of dealing with his own children and their genital curiosity and their emerging sexuality that will constitute a significant improvement over the way in which *he* was treated.

It seems to me that, as the new mode of internal control of sexual behavior begins to emerge, a three part obligation presents itself to society-at-large: society should offer to youth whatever information it requests regarding sex; it should then provide youth with freedom to experiment; and finally, it should stand ready to help pick up whatever pieces fall to the ground when the occasional drastic mistake blows off the roof. As has been pointed out, the second of these obligations is in fact already being met. It is true, of course, that society provides freedom to experiment sexually with a resigned shrug, or against its best judgment, or with goose pimpling apprehension; but it provides it. It is also true that, increasingly, society is meeting the third obligation, but much room for improvement remains here. Perhaps the next generation will be able to do something constructive about legislation that forbids the dissemination of contraceptive information and that makes illegal abortion so profitable for the most unscrupulous practitioners. But so far as the first obligation, the provision of knowledge, is concerned, society is little more generous than it was during the reign of Queen Victoria. We *think* we are more open and generous in teaching about sex, but we are still so self-conscious and embarrassed, in general, that our efforts are usually self-defeating. Again, perhaps, as I have intimated earlier, today's youth will find ways of teaching *their* children what they need to learn without the scruples and blushes behind which we have tried, usually unsuccessfully, to teach them.

To reinforce what I have said about the newly emerging mode of control of sexual behavior, I should like to cast a few barbs of criticism at the old externally imposed mode. For one single reason that mode has been doomed to failure since its inception, and that reason lies buried in the word suppression: discovery—feeling of guilt—suppression. That which is suppressed (and I am using the word in a general, rather than technical, sense) is, literally, pushed down; it is not obliterated. Freud spoke at great length and in many places of the inevitable "return of the repressed"—my use of "suppression" includes the technical psychoanalytic term "repression"—and common sense tells us that forces as inherently potent as those connected with concern for the body in general and the genital in particular, and with curiosity and adult sexuality, cannot forever be held down, regardless of the strength with which they were originally pushed. During the years of his growth the child experiences countless times the reappearance of the suppressed, and each time it is promptly pushed down all over again. Inescapably one comes to learn that the only way for the suppressed to reappear and to escape re-suppression is for it to take on some sort of culturally sanctioned disguise. So genital curiosity and sexual interest can be experienced through fashionable jokes, the *double-entendre*, calendar art, secret fantasy and clandestine "affairs." Concern for the body in general, and the genital in particular, can take the form of mink coats and cosmetics, plaid sports jackets and Edwardian pants, strapless bras and plunging necklines, bottled suntans and bulging muscles. Curiosity—poor, neglected curiosity—can occur in secret, or be attached to trivia (How many people do crossword puzzles drive to dictionaries?) or to projects of questionable social usefulness (What are the motivational factors that lead more people to buy Brand X than Brand Y? or, How much do you suppose it will cost us to get to the moon?). Because of guilt and its product, suppression, bodies are preened, but not respected. Sex is made fun of by the impotent and the frigid. And curiosity—perhaps the noblest attribute of man—is relegated to the mud of the alley, the triviality of the drawing room, the manipulations and exploitations of the market place.*

And yet another criticism comes to mind: no matter how willing the victim of suppression, deep in his heart he knows that he is right and the suppressing authority wrong. He *is* concerned for the welfare of his body, he *is* interested in sex, he *does* have curiosity, regardless of what "they" say is right or wrong. Out of this deep and pervasive realization grows, inevitably and relentlessly, a feeling of contempt for "them," a sense of conflict with society, an alienation from his human fellows, from his species-mates. It is more than possible that this realization can be carried to the point of delinquency or criminality; or it can go to the other extreme and be

* See footnote, p. 86.

forcibly denied (again, not obliterated), the individual trying, with varying degrees of success, to convince himself that "they are right, I am wrong, I will do whatever they want me to do." In short, the old externally imposed mode of control was difficult to maintain, extremely costly, and hair-triggered with dangers. Those who fought it ran the risk of futile, self-defeating, and bloody rebellion, and those who went along with it risked reducing themselves to sheep. The new mode can hardly help being better.

Before closing this chapter I should like to comment on two aspects of sexuality that have been treated with more than their share of nonsense: masturbation and homosexuality. The human being, in common with all other mammals, comes equipped with sexual organs that are arranged, in part, externally. These external parts are richly supplied with nerve endings capable of evoking sensations of pleasure when stimulated. They can be stimulated in various ways, but the pleasurable response remains about the same. In other words, the response is specific, the mode of stimulation is not. The human, again in common with all other mammals, also possesses an intricate complex of glands of internal secretion associated with the sexual system, and once these glands have reached maturity, at puberty, their hormones serve to institute periodically the physiological basis for feelings of sexual desire. In most other mammals this glandular activity occurs with marked periodicity—female dogs, for example, know sexual desire only twice a year, for about three weeks each time, and mature male dogs, for the most part, appear to feel sexual desire only when in the presence of a bitch in heat. In the human, however, the glandular activity occurs in the female once every month, and while sexual desire is without question related to that glandular process it is not, in the human, exclusively related to it. In other words, the human female is probably most

likely to feel sexual desire at about the mid-point between two menstrual periods, at the time of ovulation,
in response to her hormones. But she can also feel
sexual desire at any other time during the cycle, in
response to stimuli other than glandular. And in the
human male there is even less visible connection between sexual desire and glandular activity; sexual desire
can be aroused at almost any time, by a variety of
stimuli. It is as if, in the human animal, the glandular
activity necessary for sexual desire can be initiated at
any time, on demand.

Since sexual desire is so easily triggered in the human
being, and since its occurrence is not limited by the
calendar, it follows that periods of desire can occur
when no opportunity exists for satisfaction in the "normal" fashion, with sexual intercourse. And obviously
this is the rule, rather than the exception, in any society
in which intercourse is officially precluded until after
marriage. Unfortunately for the youth in such a society,
the highest frequency of occurrence of sexual desire
is during the years of youth and early adulthood.
Obviously, masturbation provides a way of partial satisfaction of the sexual desire that keeps cropping up, and
its use in this fashion is a normal and virtually uni-
versal human phenomenon. It provides partial satisfaction of sexual desire, of which it can relieve the
physiological aspect, but it does nothing much for the
accompanying emotional aspect, the desire for a partner
of the opposite sex with whom to share sexual union. It
can, of course, be overdone, and it can also be foregone;
and in neither extreme will any physical damage result
to the individual concerned. In the person who chooses
never to resort to masturbation there will be times when
sexual desire is strong enough to demand some degree of
satisfaction, and this is readily enough achieved, without any conscious willing, during sleep. For boys it takes
the form of the well-known "wet dream," or nocturnal

emission, and for girls (including virginal girls) it is the sometimes very vivid dream of sex play or intercourse. Contrary to much old popular belief, masturbation does not cause pimples—they result, in part, from the hormonal changes of adolescence, prior to the establishment of stable, mature glandular activity—nor does it cause insanity or impotence or frigidity. Such dire results can arise from the guilt associated with masturbation or sexual desire; if such guilt is strong enough, the resulting suppression may be so enduring that successful adult sexual functioning will be precluded, and this can be so unnerving that mental illness results. But this is a consequence of guilt and suppression, not of masturbation.

The sense of guilt attached to masturbation is sometimes of truly monumental proportions. There are young people, of both sexes, to whom masturbation is by far the most guilt-provoking sexual behavior imaginable, and in order to avoid such crippling guilt they will turn to promiscuous intercourse with whomever is available.[5] For these unfortunate people such an alternative, despite its obvious dangers, is actually less guilt-laden than masturbation. Others—again, of both sexes —turn to homosexual relationships in order to avoid the guilt of masturbation. But this is not the main cause of homosexuality, and indeed homosexual activity for the purpose of escaping the guilt of masturbation is probably rare.

Volumes have been written on the subject of homosexuality, but very little has been said concerning the fleeting and temporary homosexual-like relationships that occur fairly commonly during youth. Since the very word "homosexual" has such drastic implications, and since a good number of young people experience these fleeting and anything-but-drastic relationships, they warrant at least a brief discussion. Toward the end of the social stage of growth, as puberty approaches, boys team up with boys and girls with girls, frequently, if not usually, in best-friendships, in intimate groupings of two or three. Much of the discussion that occurs in these relationships is sexual in content, the children involved comparing notes about what each has learned, picked up, or guessed at on the subject of grown-up sexual behavior. This is an obvious precursor for puberty and the onset of the sexual stage of growth: these children are getting ready, as best they can, for the next step. Most of their dealings with each other are carried on in secret, they are frequently almost inseparable, and all in all their general behavior suggests that of adult lovers—except that no sexual activity takes place between them, and they are of the same sex.

With the arrival of puberty they drift apart and begin to learn something of the opposite sex, and they take to their early heterosexual attempts what they learned of compassion, tenderness, affection, faithfulness, friendship and emotional intimacy before puberty, with their old best friends of the same sex. There is reason to believe that this prepubertal kind of boy-boy and girl-girl relationship is an essential forerunner for later successful heterosexual relationships. But sometimes it fails to occur. If a family moves at the wrong strategic time, the prepubertal child will find himself in a strange place, where children are becoming involved with others they have known for a long time, and the newcomer may be left out, with no opportunity to prepare in this fashion for puberty. Or occasionally parents are frightened by such apparent intimacy and forbid their prepubertal children to enter such relationships. But whatever the cause, if the prepubertal experience fails to occur, it becomes a piece of unfinished business and most likely will turn up later, in another context. During the early college years, for example, one sees many girls who associate only—or mainly— with other girls, and boys with boys. Very frequently

these are young people for whom the prepubertal experiences were not possible, so they are working out the
old needs now. The very obvious difference between the
prepubertal time and middle adolescence, of course,
has to do with the intervening maturation of the
sexual system. It is not surprising that this development
casts a new light on the same-sex relationships that,
ideally, should have occurred before puberty. Frequently
they are colored by some degree of sexual behavior,
largely because the body is ready for it, partly because
it fits in so neatly with the exclusiveness, the secrecy,
the intimacy of such relationships. These are homosexual-like relationships, but the vast majority of them
are only temporary. Like their younger counterparts,
middle-adolescents leave the same-sex relationships behind and move on to heterosexuality. In short, much
of what passes for homosexuality during middle adolescence (and sometimes into late adolescence) is
nothing more than a normal developmental phase,
occurring later than it should have for best results, and
colored by physical capacities added since puberty.

****

In concluding this chapter, I should like to summarize some of what has been said. Today's young
people are discovering, or inventing, a new mode of
control of sexual behavior, despite the obstacles placed
in their path by a society that has relied perhaps too
heavily on control by guilt. Their efforts are admirable,
their results sometimes lamentable, but they can only
do what they *have* to do. They will find their way to
the necessary solutions only through experimentation
edged by dangers, and there is precious little that
we of an older generation can tell them or give them
that will be of help in their attempt. After all, they are
charting an area unknown and almost unimaginable to

us elders. For the most part, we can only wish them well. However, as a member of the left-over generation, I cannot resist the temptation to say *something*, and it is this: sex and love are two different things to start with, and the trick is to combine them. Sex without love is possible, but it is at best a mechanical mockery of what might be. And on the other side of the coin, love without responsibility is an impossibility. There is no such thing as "free" love: there is only responsible love. Two people in love, by definition, feel responsibility toward one another, and they feel responsibility toward the third person who might eventuate from their love.[6] For the girl—it is she who has the womb, who bears the baby—the consequences of love are necessarily measured in terms of the number of years it takes to have a baby and rear it. This sense of responsibility she possesses, whether she knows it consciously or not, because it is built into her. For the boy, the immediate consequences of love are of somewhat shorter duration, at first: he must learn the extent of the responsibility that stretches over the years. In practice, this means that the girl is responsible for establishing the rules, as experimentation proceeds; the boy is responsible for respecting the responsibility of the girl. To our regret, and sometimes to theirs, we of the older generation can no longer tell youth how, or where, or when to draw the legendary line; we can no longer, in good faith, tell them how to solve the sexual problems they face, because we do not know. We can only hope that youth will somehow find the answers to questions we were born too soon to recognize.

REFERENCES

1. See Chapter 2, p. 34, footnote.
2. For a detailed description of social ambiguities in this field see Margaret Mead, *Male and Female, A Study of the Sexes in a Changing World*, New York, W. Morrow, 1949, Chapter XIV.
3. Some useful books on sex are: Alan F. Guttmacher, *Babies by Choice or by Chance*, New York, Avon, 1961, and *Complete Book of Birth Control*, New York, Ballantine, 1961; R. Kempton and F. Brown, *Sex Questions and Answers*, New York, McGraw-Hill, 1950; B. R. Greenblatt, *A Doctor's Marital Guide for Patients*, Chicago, The Budlong Press, 1959 (available only through professional medical sources); Child Study Association of America, *What to Tell Your Children About Sex*, New York, Permabooks, 1954.
4. For a discussion of changing sexual ethics see Lawrence K. Frank, *The Conduct of Sex; Biology and Ethics of Sex and Parenthood in Modern Life*, New York, W. Morrow, 1961.
5. This element of guilt may explain Kinsey's finding that masturbation is more acceptable to college males and promiscuity to lower-class males. See A. C. Kinsey, W. B. Pomeroy, and C. G. Martin, *Sexual Behavior in the Human Male*, Philadelphia, W. B. Saunders Co., 1948.
6. For a detailed exposition of the relationship between love and responsibility see Fromm's *Art of Loving*, New York, Harper and Brothers, 1956.

6

Anger and Action

Much that was said in the preceding chapter about genital curiosity and sex applies as well to anger. Like genital curiosity, anger is first an experience of early childhood that is too often subjected to excessive control by guilt; and like the sexuality of late adolescence and early adulthood, anger tends to remain under the control of guilt after the need for external control has been outgrown. And in another parallel with sex, here too there is apparent substantial loosening of the cultural insistence upon control of anger during childhood, a loosening that has appeared in the course of the past quarter century.* Many people would say this loosening

* The apparent loosening of the cultural insistence upon control of anger in childhood extends also to the control of anger in adulthood, and sometimes with ludicrous results. A fashionably dressed, obviously well cared for, and presumably educated young matron was observed in a supermarket, pushing her grocery cart with her two-year-old son riding in it. At every opportunity he reached to the nearby shelves and grabbed assorted merchandise, which his mother had to dislodge from his clutching hands and replace. Finally, at the end of her rope, she slapped him and blurted, in a more-than-audible voice, "Do you have to be so damned narcissistic?" It is interesting to wonder what Freud's reaction would have been to such a popularization of his then highly unpopular teaching.

has been too much of a good thing, and those of us overexposed to young examples of the extreme in permissive* upbringing are tempted to agree. But on second thought, it is not the loosening of control over anger that sometimes makes a mockery of permissive child-rearing; that unhappy result arises, rather, from widespread confusion between the *feeling* of anger and its *expression* in some sort of action. In other words, it seems likely that the cultural loosening of control is apparent only, that in reality children are freer now to strike out or to scream out in anger, but no freer than before to *feel* anger. It is perhaps for this reason that anger, unlike sexuality, is not yet characterized by the emergence of a new pattern of internal control—a pattern that must somehow emerge, and soon.

It seems paradoxical, if not nonsensical, to say that today children are freer to *express* anger, but no freer to *feel* anger than they were during the Victorian age. But if one observes closely the manner in which the usual parent deals with an angry child of, say, three, the paradox vanishes. As I have pointed out earlier, at this age, during the emotional stage of growth, the child is busy with the identification of his feelings. He is discovering them, or at least he is discovering that they have names and that they are experiences known to others, and he is experimenting with modes of expressing them. Among his feelings he of course finds *anger*, the emotional state that arises automatically whenever he is kept from doing something he wants to do. At three the child wants to do countless things that must be forbidden, simply for his own safety or the

---

* I am using the word "permissive" in an oversimplified and generic sense to indicate the *extreme* of permissiveness. Obviously, the enlightened parent is sometimes permissive and sometimes restricting, depending upon what the child requires at the moment. In the home I am calling "permissive" it is a mandatory rule of parental behavior to be permissive *all* the time, under *whatever* circumstances, regardless of the true needs of the child.

safety of others, so that he has ample opportunity to feel his anger. Since most of the curtailment and discipline he encounters is meted out by a parent, most of his anger is directed toward the parent; and usually the contemporary American parent, regardless of how generous he or she may be in permitting the angry child to hit or kick or bite, manages to make it pretty clear to the child that he is "hurt" by the child's anger. Not by the bite, it should be noted, but rather by the fact that the child is angry with him. This makes the parent feel unloved by the child, and consciously or not, he retaliates by threatening to stop loving the child. Here is the threat that, as was implied in the preceding chapter, underlies the establishment of guilt: "If you do that Mummy won't love you any more and then you'll be sorry, because you're still too little to get along without Mummy's love."

Before the present "enlightened" age of permissive self-expression, both the child's *feeling* of anger and the *action* dictated by it were brought under the control of guilt in this fashion, and this pattern continues to be the one used in many—perhaps in most—American homes. Probably in the permissive homes this is the pattern the child learns first, but then later he learns that the angry act is acceptable and, regrettably, sometimes even encouraged. In short, regardless of the presence or absence of the permissive parental attitude, the *feeling* of anger is suppressed by guilt. The angry *action*, if it is not suppressed, becomes detached from the suppressed *feeling,* so that, in the extreme, the obnoxious freewheeling aggressive child is admired by his bemused parents for his ability to express himself. The damage he inflicts on his playmates, their toys, and the family dog is seen neither by the child nor by his parents for what it really is: tangible evidence that the anger he feels for his parents has been suppressed and shows itself only in substitutive ways.

Discovery—feeling of guilt—suppression: the child discovers his feeling of anger toward his parents, their response makes him feel guilty, he suppresses the feeling. In the permissive household the child may suppress only feelings of anger toward parents (and probably other members of the immediate household); in the nonpermissive household he will more likely suppress feelings of anger toward anyone. In the former instance he may become an adult who feels free to lash out at the world in general, but not at anyone close by in particular; in the latter he may become an adult who is "nasty-nice" to everyone he encounters. Neither type makes very agreeable company for any length of time.

At this point I can hear the voices of skeptical parents asking, "All right, Expert, how *should* it be done?" And the answer, I suspect, is as generally unusable as it is simple: be a sufficiently secure parent, in your own sense of identity, so that you are not put off or hurt when your child is angry with you, and be sufficiently aware of the fact that the world is populated by other people with whom your child has to learn to live so that you can lay on the punitive flat of the hand when it is indicated. In other words, put the horse before the cart. Let the child know it is not just all right, but inescapable, to feel anger even—or maybe I should say especially—toward a parent, but it is anything but all right for him to express it in destructive action. After all, anger can be expressed very satisfactorily, and often surprisingly constructively, in words. It does not have to be emphasized with toothmarks on Mother's thigh. A parent can say, "I know you are angry, but I can't let you bite me."

But to come back to youth in the cognitive stage of growth: as I pointed out earlier, there is nothing the young person can do at this point to change the way he was brought up. If he learned to suppress his anger toward his parents under the veil of guilt, and he probably did, at least now he has the opportunity to unlearn it, to free himself from the bondage of that particular guilt, to learn how to utilize constructively the anger he cannot escape feeling when his way has been blocked. And no more now than then is it necessary to leave scars on parental skin to prove his freedom. This is a particularly good area for the deliberate search for unfinished business, for two reasons. First, virtually every young person has some pattern of misuse or non-use of anger that he can identify with little effort. He occasionally finds himself unaccountably or disproportionately angry with a friend, or a teacher, or the boss, or even a stranger—a salesperson, perhaps. By "unaccountably or disproportionately" I mean, of course, that his anger appears without apparent reason, or that there is a reason but his response to it is greater than seems indicated. If he does not recognize this pattern in himself he will find another, a pattern of consistently *not* feeling angry when the situation dictates that he should. Secondly, each youth knows his parents well enough to recognize their patterns of anger and response to anger and to guess, with considerable accuracy, how they must have reacted to his anger when it was directed toward them. A little reflection in these two areas will undoubtedly shed some light on his own pattern, and if he works at it enough he will certainly find some sort of cause-and-effect relationship between his parents' attitude toward anger and his own. The matter may be complicated by the fact that he has one parent who over-reacted and another who under-reacted, so that perhaps in consequence he finds in himself one pattern of anger toward males and another toward females, or some other mixture of patterns. In any event, it is almost axiomatic that during youth one can discern some variety of cause-and-effect relationship between his parents' attitude toward anger, when he was little, and his own, now.

One point needs particular stress at this juncture. While it is more than likely that one's present patterns of dealing with anger were developed in a context in which one felt anger toward one's parents but was limited in expressing it, or worse, in one's freedom to feel it, it is the *patterns* that are of importance now, not the original butts of one's wrath. In other words, when the young one was three or four his mother probably saw to it, however inadvertently, that he felt guilty when he should have felt justifiably angry with her. Her attachment of guilt to his honest feeling of anger *then* is causing him a considerable degree of trouble and growing pains *now*, but he is no longer *really* angry with her for whatever was at issue then. As he tries to unravel the threads of his patterns of anger he will— and he should, if he is successful—find himself feeling waves of wrath toward his hapless parents. Under these circumstances it is good for him to remember that he is trying to make up for lost time, that the time is irretrievably lost, and that what he is feeling angry about is long since over and done with. Of course, his parents may be in his way now, he may be currently feeling entirely justifiable anger toward them, but with a little care and attention the two can be distinguished. If his anger toward the parents carries with it a sense of futility, an idea that no matter how wrong they are or how right he is nothing can be done, the chances are that he is responding to his own early history. This, of course, is the nature of the child's anger—there is, in fact, nothing he can do about it (beyond expressing it) since he is small and dependent and they are large, powerful, and the providers of care and sustenance. If, on the other hand, his current feeling of anger toward his parents is coupled with some idea, practical or fantastic, about a constructive path of action for him to take at his present almost-ripe and not really very dependent age, the odds are that his anger is truly *current* and not the product of earlier unfortunate experiences. In short, it is his right to object now to undue parental restrictions on his present behavior, and to be angry with them if they persist in telling him, for example, that at nineteen he cannot stay out past eleven o'clock on a Saturday night. It is *not* his right to set fire to their house now, simply because it has suddenly come to him that they limited his ability to feel angry with them when they kept him from experimenting with matches at the age of four and a half.

The foregoing comes under the heading of "discovery of unfinished business." Along with the discovery the young person will feel the need for experimenting, and as before this will require the exercise of a certain amount of courage. If he has been responding to the offensive manners of his roommate with an increasing display of good will and self-effacement instead of a dash of straight talk, it is fairly obvious that the time has come to try the straight talk. If he has been brought up to be "pleasant," to avoid the direct approach (and the majority have been), levelling with the roommate will be a difficult and anxiety-provoking assignment. But in no other or less painful fashion can he come to terms with the old upbringing. This is experimentation toward growth, in the clearest possible way, and it is well worth both the try and the anxiety that the try generates. Almost without exception, such an effort brings about a new openness, a marked increase in honesty and ease of communication with the roommate, a basis upon which at least a reasonable compromise between the ways of the two people involved can be established. In the absence of the experimental effort the old ways prevail: one pushes, the other gives way, and the distance between the two becomes ever wider until, finally, the gap between them *must* be recognized, usually catastrophically.

It is probably the rule, rather than the exception, that

as one experiments with the direct verbal approach to
the objects of his anger he will be temporarily carried
away and overdo it. This is one of the extremes I mentioned earlier as being characteristic of any experiment,
and it need be only temporary. If I may be allowed a
personal example, it was not until I found myself a
young and very green medical officer in the army, soon
after World War II, that I managed to attempt my
own experimentation in this regard. Generally eager to
please those in positions of authority, I began by feeling
respectful toward officers of higher rank, and since I
was a lieutenant this meant most of the rest of the
officer corps. My initiation into the world of experiment, and the anxiety it arouses, came without warning
in the middle of a summer morning soon after I had
finished the daily sick call in a field dispensary, serving
a few thousand infantrymen in arduous field training.
At the side of the room, on stretchers, lay five or six
soldiers, too sick to return to duty, waiting for an ambu-
lance to evacuate them to a field hospital. One of them
—by far the sickest—was unconscious and appeared to
have a collapsed lung. At this point into the dispensary
strode a colonel, the commanding officer of the post
(not a doctor), followed by his train of aides in single
file, arranged according to descending rank. The colonel
asked who was in charge and I presented myself, salut-
ing as best I could, and identifying myself by name,
rank, and title—Acting Post Surgeon. Pointing to the
men on stretchers with his swagger stick, he demanded
that they be got out of the dispensary immediately and
back to duty, since they were, in his eyes, nothing but
"goof-offs." I started to explain their medical plight to
him, politely and even subserviently, when he cut me
short with some remark about relative rank—I was a
lieutenant, he a colonel, and he would brook no in-
subordination. At that moment I blushed from head to
foot, burst into a cold sweat, and felt my hands shake

as I broke the bonds of my conventional middle-class Protestant upbringing. I was only a lieutenant, but I was a *doctor*, and in fact I was the *only* doctor on the post, and suddenly I knew that whatever the cost, I was a doctor first and a soldier second. Pulling myself together in a less-than-creditable fashion, and speaking past my shaking anxiety in a high-pitched, thin, altogether uncontrollable voice, I informed the colonel that I was the doctor, that those men were too sick to return to duty, and that whenever I needed his advice concerning how I should practice medicine I would come to his office and put my caduceus on his desk. (The caduceus is the identifying insignia of the army medical officer.) Thunderstruck, and literally purple in the face, he stood immobile for a moment, then turned abruptly without a word and led his aides from the dispensary. When the last and the least had finally disappeared through the door I began breathing again, although not very competently, and received the respects of my incredulous enlisted medical corpsmen who had witnessed the affair. Needless to say, I spent the rest of the day planning my defense in the theatrical court-martial I could imagine with no difficulty at all.

A little less than two years later, toward the end of my military career, I was, to the army's despair, perhaps the most aggressive reverse-action martinet in the European theater, always looking forward to the chance to go out of my way to dress down a superior officer who had the temerity to tell a doctor how to behave. Fortunately, the army and I parted peacefully. The automatic two-years-of-active-duty program separated us before the extremes of my experimental course did me in, and soon afterward I began to discover, gradually, how to temper the process.

In some respects this is not a good example. Mine was an *extreme* extreme, a little too far over on the rebellious side for best results, partly because my experimentation came later than it might have, so there was more lost time to be made up; but in addition to illustrating the extremes and the anxiety that accompany experimentation, the story demonstrates the value of beginning one's growth earlier, rather than later. The unnecessary passage of time, once emergence has become a fact, only makes the process more painful and more hazardous.

As I have said, most of American youth have been brought up in such a way that their anger in general tends to be suppressed, so that in experimenting they need to make a deliberate effort to *be* angry when they *feel* angry. Others—a minority, but a sizable one—are already angry, and have been for quite a long time, and their anger is probably directed toward almost anyone who crosses their paths. They may not at first recognize this as anger; they may believe themselves to be righteously indignant, or to be standing up for their own rights, or to be the hero who bucks City Hall. If they are convinced that they themselves are right and "they," all of them, wrong, they have an urgent need to examine their own past and the ways they have experienced anger, most particularly at home. In all probability a large measure of their hostility is no more than a disguised and constantly recurring version of ancient anger once felt toward parents but now turned against the world, more or less diffusely, in order to evade the guilt of being angry with one's parents. And regardless of the rationalization used, sooner or later they will be able to recognize in their apparent crusade an underlying sense of futility, of really being unable to do anything about it at all. Experimentation for these young people must be very nearly the opposite of what it is for the others: they have to try to check their too-easy rise of anger long enough to appraise the situation at hand objectively and dispassionately. Does this person *really* make me mad? Or am I reacting in a hostile manner out of old habit, out of an old conviction that every authority is as difficult to deal with as the first authority was? This variety of experimenting, too, is marked by extremes and flavored with anxiety. If one is a good experimenter he will find himself acting, temporarily, in a too-tractable and congenial fashion; and he will find himself surprisingly fearful and anxious the first few times he is able to avoid lashing out in the old way, without thinking. Eventually, however, he will also be surprised at how many people in authority are reasonable, and how very many more there are who not only harbor toward him no ill will but who, in fact, neither know nor care that he exists.

What I have said so far about the discovery of and experimentation with anger pertains primarily to unfinished business. Once this effort has been got under way it becomes necessary to examine the *new* business of anger, new because of the new capacities that come with the cognitive stage of development. Probably the most important of these new capacities, at least with regard to anger, is the one that makes it possible for the budding adult to be a member of the whole human race. Prior to emergence he was only a member of the family. When he was angry it was because his *own* way was blocked. Now he has the ability to feel anger when someone else's way is blocked, and this is a development with far-reaching implications; but he will be able to *use* this new ability only after he has discovered how to use his own personal anger, without the coloration of guilt. Using the new ability involves, for example, feeling angry when the way of a Negro is blocked in the deep south, when a Jew is denied housing in a restricted area, when thousands of Asians die of hunger because nobody will find a way to give them some of our surplus food, when Arab refugees hunger and stagnate in camps because Politics prevents their rehabilitation. On the home-town scale its use involves feeling

angry when one sees a bully beating a child, an employer
mistreating an employee, an obvious miscarriage of
justice, a slum landlord growing fat on the misery of
his tenants.

But using the new ability involves more than just
feeling anger. Recognizing the feeling comes under the
heading of "discovery of new business": once again,
discovery needs to be followed by experimentation.
And here, unfortunately, there is little precedent to
follow, few examples to use as guides to one's own
efforts, not much foundation provided by one's elders
upon which to build a way of one's own. We have been
called a complacent nation, a country of "fat cats"
occupied only with our own interests. The charge is
justified, to some degree, and partly because we seem to
have lost the ability to complain about the many facets
of our world that need to be complained about. The
youthful generation has been called the complacent
generation and the silent generation. Having spent a
good deal of time listening to some of its members I
disagree that they are, as a generation, complacent;
certainly they are much less complacent than their
elders appear to be. But they *are* silent: they seem not
to know what to do with their complaints, their angers,
their well-founded objections to some of the ways the
world is being run. It is in this area of *action* based
upon *anger* that they have to experiment.

I suspect the chances of youth to free anger from
guilt, to make it a potentially constructive force, are
much greater than were the chances of their parents;
and I suspect, too, that the young will be better than
their elders at discovering ways to utilize that force.
How they will do it I do not know. Doubtless it will
involve speaking out, making their discontents known,
demanding change where they feel change is needed. If
we can predict on the basis of the ways of youth in
other countries, countries in which the voice of youth

has been traditionally a force for change, political and otherwise, it will probably also involve some form of organization. But whatever youth works out, they will get to it only by way of extensive experimentation based upon the new-found ability to feel a more than personal anger without guilt.

In this context I must mention that a new form of guilt, a constructive variety of guilt, can now be discerned. This is the guilt felt by the mature person who witnesses an act of injustice—say, a bully beating a child—and who fails to act on the feeling of anger such a scene evokes within him. Unlike the old guilt, which arises simply because one feels angry and anger is not supposed to be felt, this new guilt arises when one feels honestly and appropriately angry and fails to act accordingly. It constitutes an inherent signal for positive action, rather than for cringing. It arises from the depths of one's own awareness, rather than from some long-remembered dictum of society. Its conspicuous absence in masses of people who are adult only in the chronological sense makes for a great deal of man's inhumanity to man. Were it not for that absence, that indifference, there could never have been a successful Capone, or Hitler, or McCarthy, and maybe not even radioactive fallout.

A word of caution needs to be inserted here. There have always been professional angry people who translate their anger into what they believe to be constructive action, but too often they are people who have not first taken care of the old unfinished business. In consequence, their wrath, which frequently seems aimed in a humanitarian direction is, in reality, substitutive or compensatory. They are taking it out on the world, as they probably in childhood took it out on the family dog. Since their motives (which they do not see) are juvenile, their results are too often destructive in the long run. Sometimes, of course, and largely by accident, their efforts have a constructive outcome; but it is only the thin line of fate that separates a McCarthy from a home-town reformer. As always, unfinished business needs to be cared for before the way is clear for the new.

At the beginning of this chapter I mentioned that anger, unlike sexuality, is not yet characterized by the emergence of a new pattern of internal control, in contrast to the old mode of externally imposed control by guilt. Now it is evident that another fundamental difference exists between the handling of sexuality and the handling of anger. By control of sexuality I mean the imposition of limits of its consequences; but by control of anger I mean just the opposite, the *utilization* of its consequences. It is interesting to note that in our corner of the world, where both sex and anger have been under the grip of guilt, we have developed a society that is widely known for its over-utilization of the fringes of sex—as in movies, literature, advertisements—and just as widely known for its *under*-utilization of anger.[1] We are the nation, for example, that wants everyone to like us; we are the people which has elevated popularity to the level of a status symbol. And yet, paradoxically, we seem to revel in the wrath of others. Note, for example, the fantastic amount of violence in our TV diet. If we have gained ground in our acceptance of the reality of sex since Freud's day, we have lost ground in our acceptance of the equal reality of anger. Once we were angry enough to issue a ringing Declaration of Independence and then to fight our way through the Revolution; now we hardly even write letters to editors, much less to our congressmen. But at the deviant edges of our society there is juvenile delinquency of sobering proportions and an extraordinary wealth of crimes of senseless violence. It seems incontrovertibly clear that anger is escaping the outmoded and inadequate control-by-guilt, and escaping it most dangerously. Obviously much work is cut out for youth. New patterns of utilization of anger need to be developed, and it is up to the new generation to find them. They will have more difficulty learning to live with anger than they will with sexuality, and globally speaking, at least, the importance of the former greatly outweighs that of the latter.

REFERENCES

1. It is also interesting to note that sex and aggression (or anger) were the two great "instincts" posited by Freud. He saw, with the unprecedented clarity of vision of the truly creative, that time and again people were driven by sex and/or aggression, that these were the forces that, above and beyond all others, contributed to the development of neurosis. He believed these instinctual forces to be aspects of the animal in man, of the deeply unconscious Id, and felt that the best that could be done with them was to harness them into some sort of useful compromise, through the not too successful instrumentality of the Ego, with the harsh and inescapable demands of the Superego. Now it seems increasingly apparent that the manifestations of sex and aggression that he took to be instinctual in nature were only the unfinished business of infancy and childhood, carried over unchanged and undealt with into adulthood, returning incessantly—"the return of the repressed"—to plague their possessors who were adult in years only.

It appears to me most likely that it is this change in definition of the nature of the old Freudian concepts of sex and aggression that has given rise, however implicitly, to the new ego psychology. If these two forces are really unfinished business, rather than instinctual, then the potentiality of the ego to deal with them is vastly greater than was formerly believed. If they are unfinished business rather than instinctual, then something substantially better and greater than mere compromise is possible, the ego is much more powerful in its own right than it was earlier believed to be, the id is more human nature than the incarnation of evil, and the superego is nothing more than an idol with feet of clay.

But in fairness to Freud it must at the same time be pointed out that it was his method, his unswerving, intellectually honest, tenacious questioning of that which was not to be questioned, that has made it possible for us, during the past half century, to explode the myths he inherited, and the myths he inadvertently created as well. It is a truly great body of theory that so expands knowledge that the theory itself is vanquished and superseded. Freud was not just a generation ahead of his time—he was more nearly a century ahead. He wrote, "Where Id was, there shall Ego be" (New Introductory Lectures). Had he survived only a little longer, it is conceivable that he would also have written, "Where *Superego* was, there too shall Ego be."

The young people with whom I have been professionally associated, and who have been my unwitting teachers, have consistently transmuted the instincts of sex and aggression into mere unfinished business, and they have then gone on to finish the unfinished. In the process, Id and Superego both seem to be swallowed up by Ego, which then becomes something very much greater than the sum of its parts—perhaps the final result should be called the Self.

7

Anxiety and Growth

Sex and anger, as we have seen, are realities of life that have traditionally been subjected to control by guilt. We have seen, too, that such control is not entirely successful, that it is emotionally expensive, and that it is, in reality, an *externally* imposed mode of control that is all too likely to break down in deviant and unexpected ways. True, when a person transgresses he feels guilty and the feeling is obviously *inside* him, but the definition of right and wrong which he has transgressed is not his definition—it was established for him by someone else. But by the time youth is reached one is old enough to establish one's own definitions, based on one's own experience (and experimentation), and consequently to replace the externally imposed control by guilt with an internal mode of control more precisely fitted to one's own needs, capacities, and limitations. Finally, we have seen that a new mode of internal control of sexuality seems to be arising in the youthful generation and that the time is ripe for the development of a new mode of control of anger. Unfortunately, however, we cannot stop here. Creditable—and difficult—though it is to learn one's own modes of controlling sexuality and anger, these are not enough. Another major area remains to be freed from hampering external control, and that area is *anxiety*.[1]

It is interesting to note in passing that in Freud's view of man (I have mentioned earlier the similarity of this view to the Protestant notion of imperfect man) the individual is driven by the two basic and powerful instincts[2] of sex and aggression, and is checked by the opposing and inhibiting demands of society. In such a view the individual hardly seems to have a mind of his own. He has instincts which generally tend to cause trouble, and the rules, regulations, customs, and taboos of society tend to tame them enough so that open warfare is avoided. Somewhere between the instincts and civilization stands the hapless and nearly choiceless individual, and about the best he can do with his own mind is to effect some sort of compromise between the extremes. This cannot be achieved without heavy and consistent reliance on guilt as a controlling mechanism—it is through guilt that society, or civilization, controls—and the price the individual pays for his compromise is measured in terms of neurosis. Society says the instincts are Bad (although at the same time society admits that some of their consequences are Good). Since Man is dependent upon society and must meet its views he feels obediently guilty whenever one of the "bad" instincts attempts to reveal itself, and "everybody" is "neurotic."

At least this scheme is a tremendous improvement upon the earlier fatalistic notion that one's life is predetermined and its outcome already inscribed in a big book in heaven. On that basis the individual had no choice at all in the way he lived his life. If he was born a slave, he died a slave. If his father was a cobbler, he was a cobbler. If he was born a sinner he died a sinner. The Freudian view at least gives the individual the right, and the responsibility, to work out the best and least limiting compromise he can between his inborn imperfections and the perfectionistic demands of society. And in the Freudian view man's imperfections are, primarily, sex and aggression—both generally called bad by society.[2]

It is not difficult to understand how sex and aggression, in the nineteenth century, came to be known as instincts that drive men. Society held that they were bad, so they were suppressed, but they kept cropping up, "returning," so often and so consistently that it would have been difficult indeed to see them as anything but primary forces that shape and color all human behavior. Now, however, a half century after Freud, society is not nearly so convinced that sex is generally bad, and it seems uncertain about the badness of aggression, or anger. As a result of this liberalizing of the societal view, the old pattern of discovery—feeling of guilt-suppression appears to be giving way to the growth sequence discovery—experimentation—mastery. As I have noted, the change is more marked and visible with respect to sexuality than to anger, but even concerning the latter it is a real change. It is making possible the slow emergence of a new and revolutionary view of man, a view that holds that he is born not imperfect but rather incomplete, and that his completion is his own business, his own responsibility, his own right.

Anxiety is also subject to external control by guilt. Perhaps it follows, then, that anxiety, like sexuality and anger, can be freed of guilt and allowed to participate in the growth sequence of discovery—experimentation—mastery. I am convinced that this is, indeed, the case; that the young person can find a way to liberate his anxiety, to identify it, experiment with it, learn to use it—in short, he can achieve his own internal control of it. With regard to sexuality youth is already doing this.

With regard to anger, youth is about to achieve it, although with a good deal of difficulty. In the case of anxiety such internal control may be even more difficult to achieve, but the importance of the effort may well be even greater.

I have described anxiety earlier[3], but one point remains to be added: since anxiety is most often a state of emotional discomfort, it is usually considered, at least in our society, to be a state of *unhappiness*. Now we can begin to see the dilemma posed by anxiety. It is the normal emotional response to anything new, unexplored, or uncharted—and the growing child is an inveterate explorer. But anxiety is equated with *unhappiness*, and nothing is more un-American than unhappiness. If this seems too sweeping a statement one need only look at a few advertisements and commercials. The people in them are invariably happy people, and the products they promote, without exception, promise to increase, or at least to maintain, the happiness of the purchaser. One may also observe parents of young children, and note the urgency with which they attempt to change a temporarily unhappy child into a happy one. The preamble to the Constitution guarantees the right to the *pursuit* of happiness; we have too broadly misinterpreted this as the right to the *possession* of happiness. All our folk heroes live *happily* ever after; the goal of marriage is conjugal *happiness*; a new dishwasher, or a mink coat, will make Mother happy, a bar in the basement will make Daddy happy, and tranquilizers—"Happy Pills"—comprise about 50 per cent of the output of the American drug industry, and make its stockholders happy. But the anxious child is seen as an unhappy child; it is bad to be anxious and make Mummy unhappy, so in order to be considered good the child learns to suppress his anxiety under the rule of guilt. Unfortunately, however, control by guilt is not the only force that encourages the suppression of anxiety, nor is it the most important one. Anxiety is also subjected to control by *fear*.

I have described anxiety as a sense of tension, almost always tinged with fear; there is no question but that fear itself is a variety of unhappiness, and further, a variety that everyone avoids as much as possible. There is also no question but that some new experiences are fear-inspiring. The eighteen-month-old toddler who falls into the deep end of a swimming pool for the first time will be scared for some time after he has been fished out, and with good reason. But the same toddler placing a box on a chair, then climbing up and standing atop the rickety tower for his first view of the top of the mantel, will not be scared. He will feel some degree of anxiety simply because he has tried something new, and it will be so minimal that only a rather skilled observer will be able to identify it—unless, that is, his mother suddenly comes in from the kitchen, sees him on his precarious perch, and emits a frightened maternal shriek. If she is that scared, he too will be scared; and if enough of his early exploratory attempts meet the same kind of parental reaction, it will not be long before his anxiety is consistently tinged with fear, whether or not the object of his exploration is inherently fearsome. In other words, it seems entirely probable that at first the child—any child—is a fearless explorer, except when his explorations bring him into contact with something that is genuinely fear-inspiring; but as time passes he is too often taught to equate *all* explorations with fear. If he learns this lesson thoroughly, he will react with tension-tinged-with-fear to almost any new experience; his parents will probably think his fears are evidence of unhappiness, and they will do what they can to make him happy once again. If they, in their turn, are successful, they will soon have a child who is afraid of new experiences, afraid to explore, afraid (worst of all) of his own *anxiety*, the feeling that lets him know he is confronting something new.

At the other extreme is the individual who has *not* learned to equate anxiety with fear. When he encounters something new (assuming it is not inherently dangerous or threatening) he too reacts with the physical changes associated with the body's preparation for action: increased heart rate, rapid and shallow breathing, tightening of muscles, perspiration, often a trembling of the hands. But if these changes are not accompanied by a feeling of fear, we are more likely to say that the person is feeling excitement or heightened interest or active curiosity than to say that he is experiencing *anxiety*. In other words, it seems very probable that the element of emotional discomfort that we usually consider an inherent part of anxiety is, for the most part, learned. (After all, most of the new experiences we discover are not only not inherently dangerous —they are downright inviting.) Obviously this is not true of the anxiety one feels when facing a genuinely threatening situation, and probably it is not true, either, of prolonged anxiety, whether its source is threatening or not. But it does appear to be true of most of the day-by-day anxiety we experience in the process of growth.

To summarize, then, anxiety is the normal emotional response to anything new or unexplored; it need be accompanied by a feeling of fear only when the new is in some way inherently dangerous; because of parental and/or societal teaching it is much too frequently accompanied by fear whether the new is dangerous or not, and since it seems to constitute unhappiness it is also guilt-provoking. When it occurs without fear or guilt it is indistinguishable from excitement or heightened interest and it leads directly to exploration of, or experimentation with, the new; and when it is needlessly tinged with fear and guilt it tends to prevent exploration or experimentation. In other words, anxiety uncontaminated with needless fear leads to growth, while anxiety associated with irrational fear prevents growth. Most American young people have been taught to associate anxiety with fear and to control their anxiety with guilt. As long as such a control is operative, growth toward maturity is difficult indeed.

Before I criticize the parental generation for planting such a bad seed so soon, however, I should point out that the very first *new* experience encountered by the human baby is inherently dangerous, so that the first anxiety is inevitably flavored with fear. This first frightening experience is related to separation from the mother. The newborn baby cannot distinguish between himself and his setting. When he has developed enough to make the distinction he encounters the new possibility that he may be separated from his mother, and at so young an age such a possibility is threatening indeed. The seed is planted on fertile soil: the *first* anxiety is fear-ridden; it is easy enough to decide that *all* anxiety is fear-ridden, to reinforce the content of fear in that first anxious experience. The question now is, how does one purify his anxiety? How free it from needless fear, how divorce it from guilt? Fortunately, the process is not significantly different from those I have discussed earlier with reference to sexuality and anger.

Once again, it is necessary to think in terms of both unfinished business and new business. Under the heading of unfinished business comes the response of his parents to the child's early exploratory ventures. If they were more cautious than wise, they were only doing what they believed to be right on his young behalf, but their well-meant efforts kept him from being the explorer he might have been. The cognitive young person might ask himself such questions as these: To what

extent did they prevent me from discovering things on
my own? Leaving guilt out of it for the moment, to
what extent did they discourage me from exploring
and experimenting during the early stages of growth,
not just because what I was about to discover was bad,
but because the act of discovering itself, involving as it
does confrontation with the new and hence the feeling
of anxiety, is bad? To what degree was I taught that
the virtues of prudence outweigh those of the gamble,
of the untested attempt? And in another vein, what
evidence can I find in myself of fear-ridden anxiety
when, in reality, no fear is indicated? Do I have consistent and repetitive patterns of anxiety, particularly
of disguised anxiety, in response to situations that
turn up time and again, in routine and inescapable
fashion, rather than a history of gradually increasing
mastery of such situations? Can I distinguish, in myself,
between *anxiety* and *excitement*? For that matter, do
I know what excites me, what interests me, what arouses
my curiosity, or do I search endlessly for something of
interest, something I can get my teeth into, or some
inexhaustible source of dangerous and titillating "kicks,"
such as drag racing? In short, at this moment in my
life am I a fearless explorer and experimenter (except
in the face of genuine danger), or do I hold back, out of
old habit, or do I court anxiety recklessly? [4]

Whatever is suppressed, whether because of guilt or
fear, returns endlessly until the suppression ends, and
it may return in all manner of disguises. It is for this
reason that anxiety so frequently occurs in camouflaged
form. It is safer and less guilt-provoking to suffer a
tension headache, or to raid the refrigerator compulsively, or to get lost in front of the television screen
or in a bar, than it is to feel plain, unadorned anxiety.
This is reflected in the old conviction, mentioned
earlier, that "everyone" is "neurotic." Many forms of
disguised anxiety at least resemble neurosis; indeed,

if the process lasts long enough, some of them actually do become neuroses. The work of Freud taught us how to begin to free sexuality and anger from the control of guilt, and now we must take the next step and teach ourselves how to free our anxiety from control by guilt and, still more important, from control by fear. Franklin Roosevelt said our greatest fear is of fear itself, and a more appropriate comment could hardly be voiced. To free our anxiety it is necessary, first, to stop fearing it; we need to learn to stop fearing what we have been taught to fear. It is this effort that brings me to a discussion of new business.

The usual youth may have a good deal of difficulty discerning the course of his anxiety through the earlier stages of growth, but he will find his current anxieties, in the cognitive stage, visible enough. At this age most young people feel anxiety to some degree and in some form much of the time. They are frequently moody, or tense, or mildly depressed, or bored, or just vaguely off-color, or worried or nervous or *something*. Anxiety is the normal emotional response to anything new, and they are facing the newness of the cognitive stage of development, the stage in which it is possible to be aware in a totally new fashion of themselves and their setting, their past and their future. Consequently they have no choice but to feel anxiety, and the first big step in mastering it is to accept it and get used to it. So long as one tries to make it go away, it can only return to plague him further; so long as he sees it as abnormal or sick or unnatural, he is fearing fear and merely postponing mastery of his own anxiety. To be blunt, he will first have to decide that his anxiety exists, that it is normal, and that he is stuck with it. Once this is accomplished, he can proceed with the effort to discover what specific new issues are stirring it up, and then experiment with them until some level of mastery is reached. Early in the course of experimenting he will note, to his pleasure, that the anxiety seems to have vanished.

Especially during the earlier years of youth, a common error occurs which prevents mastery of anxiety. This error consists of excessive communication with, and reliance upon, those to whom one's anxiety is least acceptable. The youth who telephones the old folks at home to tell them his troubles will not relieve his own misery, and he will add to theirs. Then he will feel worse than ever, because he has caused them needless trouble. For best results the young generation has to learn to suffer in silence most of the time. Of course it is useful to mention one's misery occasionally, but this can best be done with friends who are also suffering, or with adults who understand something about anxiety, rather than with adults who as parents are dedicated to protecting their young from it. Another common error is to assume that one is the *only* sufferer. Here is an opportunity for a little ready experimentation: it is easy to ask around, or at least to look around, among one's friends and acquaintances, for signs of anxiety in them. At the least this will reduce the feeling of painful uniqueness. Still another common error is the belief that one's seemingly popular and successful contemporaries, who show no discernible anxiety and appear to be consistently happy, are right and the sufferer and his fellow-sufferers wrong. True enough, the popular and successful are better suppressors, but suppression and growth do not go together. Many of the popular and successful youths of a generation ago are the perennial sophomores of today. Their empty but gaudy lives are a poor advertisement for the suppression of anxiety.

In the cognitive stage typical areas of anxiety-provoking concern are such issues as religion, philosophy, politics, authority, independence, commitment, vocational choice, dating and sex, marriage. Young people find themselves anxiously questioning all sorts of principles by which they have been brought up, principles that, by societal definition, are supposed to be beyond questioning or criticism. They are, however, principles forged by others—not necessarily in error, but hand-me-down principles, nonetheless. And if the curiosity of youth is alive they will have to be examined, in spite of anxiety. Only if the young person finds the courage to question them will he be able to know which apply to him and which must be discarded or modified; only if he questions the old principles will he be able to forge new ones, or to act on the old ones, with honesty and integrity.

Discovery—experimentation—mastery: I have referred to this as the growth sequence, and if we consider that word "discovery" for a moment it will be evident that anxiety is an inescapable element of the growth sequence and of growth itself. Discovery implies something new, anxiety is the normal emotional response to the new, therefore discovery—and *growth*—cannot occur without anxiety. But as we have seen, anxiety need not be as painful as it is popularly believed to be. If anxiety is divested of irrational fear, growing *pain* is transformed into growing *pleasure*: the new is faced with excitement, with interest, with zest, and exploration and experimentation are entered upon with eagerness. Conversely, so long as anxiety is fear-ridden, discovery itself is inhibited and experimentation too readily sacrificed to suppression. If growth occurs at all under such hampering circumstances it *is* painful, hesitant, and often incomplete.

***

To summarize the last three chapters: sexuality, anger, and anxiety are facts of life. They exist as long as life continues; they are aspects of human reality; they must be lived with. Sexuality and anger are not inherently bad, anxiety is not necessarily fearsome or an indication of unhappiness. All three can be shorn during the years of youth of the misconceptions, misinterpretations, and nonsense associated with them by society. Discovery—experimentation—mastery can be made to replace discovery—feeling of guilt (or fear)—suppression. Of these three facts of life anxiety is by far the most important; until and unless it is mastered, growth in other spheres will be, at best, incomplete. Youth is the age of anxiety. If the young can teach themselves to avoid fearing irrational fear, it can become the age of excitement, the age of interest, the age of growth.

REFERENCES

1. See Ref. 2, pp. 26-27.
2. See Ref. 1, pp. 124-125.
3. See Chapter 1, p. 5.
4. In this connection it is relevant to mention one specific form of disguised anxiety that is characteristic of only a very small minority of contemporary youth, but the dangers of which more than outweigh its rarity. This is the anxiety that takes the paradoxical form of a *denial* of anxiety: it occurs primarily among the ranks of delinquent and near-delinquent young people who seem compulsively to drive themselves into dangerous or anxiety-producing situations, to take pride in their ability to "play it cool" through such situations, only to repeat the same process over again and again. It is as if such a youth feels that he has not won his first battle

THE ART OF GROWING

with anxiety, and that he must challenge himself to that first battle over and over, incessantly. Unfortunately his guilt is so enormous, and he clings to it with such bull-dog tenacity, that he is unable to learn from his great wealth of experience. One is reminded in this regard of the alcoholic or of the financially well-fixed shoplifter. Such young people as these are fear-ridden to an extent they themselves would find impossible to believe, and their acted-out efforts to prove that their anxiety and fear do not exist place them in ever more hazardous positions. And to make matters worse, anxiety is not the only source of their difficulties. They are also unable to deal with anger—hence they are characteristically diffusely hostile and rebellious—and they know sex only as a means of manipulation, exploitation, or defiance. They are the victims of the most extreme misapplications of the Protestant ethic, and they constitute our most vivid examples of the consequences of its faults.

Conclusion

Words, somehow, seem unsatisfactory symbols to use in drawing a road map. Or perhaps the feeling of dissatisfaction stems from the fact that the road is not entirely clear to the map-maker. But in any event the deed is done and I hope that a fuzzy map is better than none at all. The road to psychological maturity is twisting, hilly, and poorly surfaced, and some people insist that it has no ending, except in death. They speak of an endless process of maturing: one is forever approaching or moving in the direction of maturity, but the goal is never reached. For these people there is a *process* of psychological maturation, but no such thing as a *state* of psychological maturity. Others insist that psychological maturity is an easily attained goal, characterized by the simple learning or imitation of suitable social roles, by the parroting of conventional cultural beliefs. I have no choice but to disagree with both views. The first confuses maturation with growth, the second confuses it with imitation. An oak tree, with a life span of perhaps two hundred years, begins as an acorn, that germinates to become a seedling. Growth continues until the seedling becomes a sapling, and continues further until the sapling becomes, unmistakably, a tree —a young tree, it is true, and a small one, but a definite tree. At this point, perhaps ten years after germination of the acorn, the oak has reached *maturity*. During the next couple of centuries it will continue to grow in size, but regardless of the majesty of its old age it will never be more *tree* than it was at ten.

Similarly, the human being, with a life span of seventy years, begins as a fertilized egg, which grows into a fetus, which is delivered as a baby, which grows through childhood and adolescence to reach physical adulthood at about age fifteen. At this point the human being has achieved *physical* maturity, and although he will grow further in size, in experience, and, we hope, in wisdom, no matter how grey his beard he will never be more essentially mature, in the physical sense, than he was at fifteen. The discrepancy in views of maturation occurs because, in the human instance, physical maturity does not coincide with psychological maturity. Some people are in a state of permanent "maturing," of slow and delayed psychological growth that is usually ended by death in old age before psychological maturity has been reached; many others are conformers or rebels, apparently in a state of no psychological growth at all. But it is possible, I insist, for the human being to achieve psychological maturity, if he works at all, within five to ten years after the achievement of physical maturity. Of course he will then continue to grow psychologically as well as to age physically; he will continue to experience the new, to learn, to change, to expand his horizons, to grow in wisdom and judgment. He will become increasingly more "alive," more interested, more curious, deeper and broader; he will become more humble, saying "I know," less often, and "I hope" and "It seems" more often. He will grow, his psychological stature will increase, but at fifty or sixty or seventy he will be no more *mature* a human specimen, psychologically speaking, than he was at twenty-five.

Psychological maturity begins when a person knows who and what he *really* is, as opposed to what he is "supposed" to be. The eternal maturer is still trying to puzzle out his own identity at sixty-five; the conformer is satisfied to act out what he is supposed to be, and the rebel to refute it. But the psychologically mature person knows who he is at twenty-five, he knows who he is at forty-five, and he still knows who he is at seventy-five. He has a sense of sameness, of continuity, of basic identity, which remains constant despite the passage of time, the variety of experience, the growing accumulation of wisdom. The perennial maturer has, for his central core, the eternal question, "Who am I?" and his life is dedicated to a never-finished search for the answer. The conformer has nothing more than his dependence upon the social context within which he is forever stuck, like a raisin in a rice pudding. His life is dedicated to maintaining the status quo, to preserving the relationship between raisin and rice. And the rebel, more like than unlike the conformer, also has nothing more than his dependence upon the social context. Where the conformer remains passive and content the rebel struggles and fights, but neither transcends the status quo. It is difficult to take seriously even a fighting raisin.

It is interesting to compare the way the world appears to each of these groups. For the psychologically mature person the world comes alive and constitutes a field within which he lives his life, and with which he himself is in constant and intimate interaction. He is virtually always aware of his world, as he is aware of himself, and his world is broad and varied, beautiful and ugly, worthy of love and hateful, his alone and yet shared with everyone else. It is his to enjoy and his to improve where he can improve it. For him the world and the self are equally real, equally identifiable, equally meaningful. For the conformer the world is a rather glutinous mass containing the exemplars of the roles he plays and the proponents of the views he parrots, and the same world exists for the rebel—but instead of playing roles and

parroting views he fights and resists. Neither the conformer nor the rebel really exists in his own eyes, in his
own right. The world exists, authority exists, but his
appraisal of *himself* comes to him only by reflection
from the eyes of others. And finally, for the perennial
maturer the world is not much more than a space within
which he carries out his never-ending search for his own
identity. He really has little to do with the world—his
energies are turned inward. In his own eyes *he* is the
fascinating enigma, and the world is peripheral and
almost, even, irrelevant.

In short, psychological maturity *can* be won; a person
can find within himself psychological normality; he can
lift himself, by his own bootstraps, above the mediocre
average. And as I have tried to indicate, he can do it in
what at least approaches a systematic fashion. Implied
throughout this book is the belief that the task can be
accomplished—and can be accomplished *only*—through
the use of the intellect. Since this, too, is an area much
bedevilled by cultural myth, a brief discussion is war-
ranted. Because we confuse the average, the mass, and
the normal, we have wrongly assumed that only the
giant can perform with excellence. There are a few great
lovers, for example, and there are all the rest of us; we
try, but we believe our efforts are really not remarkable.
There are a few great fighters, a few great workers, a few
great artists, only one Schweitzer, and again all the rest
of us. And in similar vein we assume that only the giant
can *think*. This is, of course, patent nonsense. With
exceptions that are statistically insignificant we are
all similarly equipped, even mentally—"All men are
created equal"—but we do not use our equipment
equally.

Certainly I do not hold that we can expect more
than one Schweitzer or Einstein or Da Vinci per generation. But we can, and to survive we must, expect tens
and hundreds of thousands to use their brains and their

brawn and their hearts to the fullest extent of their ability. It is no more than childish guilt, and senseless fear, and unaccepted anxiety that prevent this, and all these can be vanquished by the use of the intellect. We can no longer afford the absurd luxury of scorning the egghead, we can no longer afford to subsidize the college athlete rather than the college student, or to pay the teen-age rock 'n' roll star millions while teachers must tend gasoline pumps after school in order to feed and educate their own children. In short, we need to admit to ourselves that *thinking* is a process for men, not just for the gods. According to Brand Blanshard, a professor of philosophy, the sort of thinking we have to do is ". . . the thinking necessary to the good citizen, the good neighbor, the good father or mother of a family, the competent man of affairs, the supporter of sound causes generally, the person with sensitive allergies for political hokum, specious advertising, religious superstition, class and race tension, and lopsided partisanship in all its fifty-seven varieties . . . the difficulties are less logical than psychological. The main one is to stick to the path of reasonableness through a fog of passion, pride and prejudice, to thread one's way through a thicket of likes and dislikes, callow enthusiasms, dubious authorities and distorting complexes." [1] This, clearly, is plain *human* thinking, not godlike or "giant" thinking. We can think if we will, and if we think we can grow.

REFERENCES

1. B. Blanshard, " 'Hamlet' vs. The Laws of Thermody-
namics," *The New York Times Magazine*, Dec. 24,
1961, pp. 8, 16.

Epilogue for Parents

To many parents who have worked their way through this book I suppose I seem to be a traitor to my own generation. This I deny: I do not believe that my generation, despite its shortcomings, deserves to be treated treacherously. But at the same time I am convinced that the youthful generation needs a spokesman, someone who will speak *to* them and *for* them. Their way is not ours; we have difficulty recognizing its validity; but it is real, and it is theirs. The course of growth I have tried to illustrate in this book is not something I have made up out of the blue; it is a way of growth I have been shown by young people during the last decade, and that young people are still showing me daily. Comparing their way with ours makes it very clear that the advantage is with them: they are *trying* to grow, and to grow right; we grew, if at all, by accident, and almost in spite of ourselves. Among my own contemporaries I can find many conformers and rebels and more than a few dreamy-eyed perennial maturers, but psychologically mature specimens are few and far between. In the youthful generation I have encountered I would hazard the guess that psychological maturity is around the next corner for perhaps 15 per cent.

The parent of one of these young people has my sympathy, and his child has my respect. A grower is a difficult sort of child to have around the house. He (or she) asks many, many questions, some of them embarrassing if not downright prying. He can spot Daddy's faults mercilessly, and he can pick out Mommy's most vulnerable areas at twenty paces. He may be miserable, locked in his room playing a moody record of Wagner with the volume turned up too high, while the rest of the kids in the neighborhood are outside having a good time. Or in contrast he may come home from school deliriously singing the praises of a tough teacher who reduces most of his contemporaries to frustrated tears. He is forever experimenting, at seeming risk of life, limb, and the parental house, and his bruises and his parents' repair bills illustrate his failures and near misses. He argues, debates, criticizes, and quibbles. When he has a project under way he has no sense about such trifles as sleeping and eating, but a week later, strictly for experimental purposes, he subjects himself to the most rigid sleeping schedules and dietary regulations. He is so full of surprises that his own parents feel as if they do not know him; and when his pain is more apparent than his growth they ask in anguish, "Where have we failed?"

Yet it is with the grower, regardless of the immensity of his struggles, that we of the parental generation have *not* failed. Somehow, without really knowing what to do for him or how to go about doing it, we have managed to give him freedom enough to grow and, at the same time, protection enough to keep him alive. But we *have* failed with the conformer, the pleasant, placid, congenial child who develops in our own image, repeating our mistakes, mimicking our way of life, depending forever on our outmoded judgments, amiably accepting as gospel the principles and beliefs forged by us, or borrowed by us, a generation ago. Somehow, and again without knowing how, we have prepared the conformers for life in a world that no longer exists except in our memories and their misconceptions. And we have failed, too, with the rebels. In some mysterious fashion we have prepared them for life in a world in which the status quo must be fought, and fought, and fought, but never replaced or rebased. Somehow we have made of each rebel a latter-day Don Quixote who, without an outmoded, anachronistic, no longer relevant windmill to tilt at, feels as if he himself has no existence.

But let us not be too lugubrious about our failures. If we have been less than perfect as parents we should remember that to err is human; and we may realize, too, that very few of us, in our day, were given freedom enough to grow in the way the grower grows. The grower is not a new phenomenon, but I am convinced that our generation of parents has turned out a much higher percentage of them than has any previous recent generation. For this we can take some degree of credit, even though we do not really know how we have brought it about. And anyway, once the cognitive stage of development has been reached, the child possesses within himself the capacity to transcend his own upbringing, to make of himself a grower, regardless of his background. As I repeatedly tell the young people with whom I work, "It may be your parents' fault you're the way you are, but it's your fault if you stay that way."

We of the parental generation are victims of history. We are the last of a variety of Mohicans: we are near the end of the historical epoch during which man's chief interest and pursuit was the mastery of his external environment. Our position would probably be humorous, rather than bewildering, if we could see it from a distance. In a way, we are the Rube Goldbergs of history. We have focused almost all our energies on the building of a great and wondrous machine that would end our troubles once and for all; and despite its complications and its intricacies we believed in it. Then, to our horror, it swayed, tottered, and is now in the process of collapsing. Most of the time we can avoid seeing the cracks in its structure and listening to the clashing of its gears—especially if we work hard enough, or play hard enough, or run fast enough, or drink seriously enough. But increasingly our children see and hear, and we cannot object if they decide they should direct their lives differently from the way we directed ours. In fact, rather than objecting, we should praise them for their efforts and cheer them on, for the sake of our own grandchildren.

Where they are going, we cannot know; indeed they themselves do not know yet. But the best of them are on their way, and although we cannot give them much help, we can at least restrain ourselves from hindering them as they work out their pioneer effort. Above all else, it is our obligation to let them do their own experimenting. Perhaps I will be charged with preaching a doctrine of license, of excessive freedom—I have heard the charge before, and despite it I continue to consider myself a moralist—but without freedom to experiment there is no learning of responsibility. Obviously this freedom entails risk, certainly it is often enough overdone or abused or misused, sometimes it is unwisely offered to young people not yet ready to utilize it. But the only alternative to the risk of freedom is the swaddling cloth of overprotection. We run the risk, and some of our young people grow: we overprotect, and they are doomed to juvenility. During the past three decades or so, we have offered the young the freedom we have gradually learned that they need, but at the same time we have burdened them with some new and rather subtle forms of overprotection. Our aim seems to have been at least to minimize, and if possible to obliterate, the natural crises of life for them, to protect them, above all else, from the anxiety without which growth cannot occur.

Two common examples of this erasure of crisis will illustrate the point. Until fifteen or twenty years ago a most revealing part of the psychiatric history of any female patient had to do with her memories of her first menstrual period. Formerly this was a crisis indeed, and often it was too much of a crisis, virtually loaded with cultural nonsense that was nothing short of destructive. No psychiatrist would dream of advocating a return to the good old days when many a girl's first period was a time of psychic catastrophe. But neither can he say much for the contemporary state of affairs, when so momentous, inherently dramatic, and symbolically significant an occasion as the first menstrual period is sufficiently smothered by maternal ministrations that it stands out in the girl's memory later as hardly different from any other day in her life.

Another example has to do with the beginning of college. Here, too, is a momentous event, a change of major proportions, particularly if the youngster is going to college away from home. This is his first real step in the direction of emancipation from home, and once he takes it there can be no real or lasting turning back. The beginning of college is, or should be, a crisis. But some secondary schools have arranged the senior year in such a fashion that it very nearly duplicates the educational experience offered during the first college year, and so the crisis is softened. The scared college freshman soon discovers that his college courses are essentially the same as those he had last year, and he decides the change is not so sweeping after all. (Many parents, of course, make this sort of softening unnecessary. They lead their college-bound offspring to the campus by the hand, after doing almost all of the work of choosing the college, filling out the application forms, arranging for housing, and sometimes, even, deciding what courses he shall take.) We have not yet devised a systematic way to protect the student from the crisis of graduation, however, so he may have a chance to grow during the latter part of his senior year in college —unless, that is, he decides to get married and let good old Dad support him and his bride. If Dad comes through, another crisis vanishes, another opportunity for growth is lost.

In short, we have to give our children the freedom to grow, and we have to steel ourselves to the unhappier consequences of their experimentation. Not all of them will succeed, and those who do may pay a price that sometimes seems to us, their parents, excessive. It may help us to remember that the years of youth are characterized by a high degree of toughness and resilience, by a fast rate of recuperation, by great stamina. And it may help, too, to realize that more and more young people have the notion that anxiety is a fact of life, rather than a blight, and that honesty is a responsibility worth working for. What seems excessive to us may feel reasonable enough to them. Indeed, this may be, in the long run, the only way we, as parents, can recognize them as grownups and cease our sighs.

And in any event, when they have reached the cognitive stage of development our work as parents is essentially finished. To use a technological analogy that belongs to our generation, it is our parental obligation to raise them until they are on the launching pad, to push the button, and then to stand back, no longer needed, and watch the results. They may fly fast and far, they may lob only a few feet and fall with a thud, they may just fizzle out, a few will explode in our startled faces. But whatever they do, it is their doing now, not ours. We will of course regret our mistakes, but we must also take credit for our victories. Despite

our blind spots, despite the fact that our world seems
no longer to exist, despite our gropings and our mistakes,
we are seeing more successful launchings than our
parents did. Maybe the growers will teach us how to be
good grandparents, and maybe they will provide us with
a good world to enjoy our grandchildren in.

INDEX

158 / INDEX